A NUMBER OF-FENCES

TO BE TAKEN

INTO CONSIDERATION

Anthony Joseph Bowles

A NUMBER OF-FENCES TO BE TAKEN INTO
CONSIDERATION

Published by A1 Book Publishing UK

ISBN 9798853754010

PROLOGUE

Having spent many years working in racing there are stories which I will not mention in these memoirs as they would make people's hair curl. However, I do hope the memories and stories which I have shared will give a little insight into how a loving upbringing and hard work can help achieve so much. You may be wondering why a man in his eighties has decided to write his life story. Well let me explain. My lovely wife Elaine had been asking me to put pen to paper for many years with no success but when Chloe (my eldest granddaughter) asked me to write my memoirs, I had to have a rethink. Chloe has never been someone who reads books so after explaining to her that reading is one of the best pastimes anyone could have, what she said next really surprised me. "Grandad, if you write your life story then I promise I will read it and you will know that it will be the first book I would have read." How could I refuse that?

Born during 'the slump years' in January 1931, the middle child of three, these were very difficult times for everyone but more so for people like my dad as he was in the building trade and had to follow the work around. He would cycle for miles just to get a day's pay. However, my mum had a very different upbringing to my dad and was raised to be a lady. She was the eldest of four and had a very privileged childhood. She was not someone who could just make do or cook a nourishing meal out of bones and vegetables, so the food we ended up eating was always very strange, for example, a bowl of cherries for dinner! It wasn't her fault and she was always very loving and kind, loyal to her children and she loved playing her piano which went everywhere with us. I remember we didn't really have much in the way of furniture but we always had the 'baby grand'. I often look back and think it must have been so very hard for my mum going from having everything to having nothing. Sadly, my dad was killed nearing the end of the Second World War while on duty in Italy. I do know that had he returned from the war then my pathway could have been very different. He always used to talk to me about how he would have a construction business after the war and he and I would do the manual work and my brother Pat would do the designing. If that had happened then maybe my memoirs would not have been so interesting or maybe it would have been a bestseller!

EARLY YEARS

Being born into this world on January 17th 1931 during a very cold winter's day, it was not a good time for anyone, least of all my dad. He was a master bricklayer and with it being the 'slump years', work was at a minimum. Consequently, during my early childhood right up until Dad joined up for the war, we moved house regularly enabling him to look for business. Mum's dad, Joseph Kelly, was a racehorse trainer and also owned a pub and this lifestyle makes me reflect on Mum and Dad's relationship. My mum must have really been in love with my dad to leave the comfort of what she had to having virtually nothing!

I was born in Gillingham, Kent on a Saturday and I do believe the old saying is true as I have always worked hard for my living. I had an elder brother Patrick and then the following year my sister Ann was born. My mum, Cecily Kelly, met my dad Leonard Bowles in her dad's pub called 'The Lisle Castle' in Kent. Grandad had bought this pub for my gran, as being a racehorse trainer, he travelled the country a great deal and therefore thought it would keep her occupied. Because Mum wasn't working for a living, other than spending a short time as a seamstress apprentice, she always used to sit at the bar looking pretty. This is where my dad fell for her. Dad used to go to the pub regularly and my grandad started to notice that they were both smitten with each other. Typical reaction of my grandad, he asked Dad into his office one day and questioned him as to who his parents were. My dad told him he knew who his mum was but never knew his dad. That was not the news that Grandad wanted to hear so he told him to get out and never come back.

When Mum heard about this, she packed her bags ready to leave. Grandad called her into his office and gave her an ultimatum. He offered to set her up in business and give her £400 if she didn't go off and marry him. This was a huge amount of money in those days, but mum told him in no uncertain terms where to go and so Grandad asked her to   leave   and   never   come   back. My dad grew up in a small country village called Oare in Kent; a very intelligent man and yet so completely the opposite to my mum (they do say opposites attract).

After Mum left home, Grandad decided to sell the pub and buy a house in College Road Epsom, still continuing to train horses in Kent. Because of the situation with my Grandad, we never got to see or visit our gran until I was about 4 years old when she would come to see us regularly without Grandad knowing. My memories of seeing my grandad for the first time was about 5 years later. I remember my gran being a lovely lady who I adored very much but Grandad being someone who wasn't interested in me at all. When Grandad bought 71 College Road his other daughter Noreen (my auntie) went with him to live there and his son Pat (my uncle) bought the house next door and later married. When Mum fell pregnant with Ann and I was almost a year-old, Noreen would come and visit us. She obviously felt the prospect of having three children was too much for my mum to cope with and asked Gran if she could take my brother Pat back to live with them. She sent Gran a telegram asking her, bearing in mind this was all done while my dad was away at work. Needless to say, when Dad came home, he was not happy about this but went along with it for Mum's sake. Soon after this, Ann also went to live with them for a while but I would never leave my mum.

I have fond memories of the 1930s; one particular memory is of seeing Dad leave for work cycling on an old bike. He must have been a real grafter but the sad thing was I didn't get to see him from one day to the next. Another of my earliest memories is riding an old tricycle in the garden then leaving the house with Mum who one day said, "Look over the road Tony, there's a black man, quickly touch your collar and wish for luck." I remember having to walk along the street one day where tarmac was fresh and I fell over. My legs had to be washed and Mum used butter to clean them and it worked! In those days children could go anywhere on their own and even before I started school I used to go to the park in Eltham. One time I went on my own during the winter and the pond had frozen over where I met some friends and we all went sliding along the bank.

I always used to go up the High Street on my own on a Saturday and watch the Punch and Judy show. I can vividly remember travelling on the tram to Woolwich. I can't remember who I went with but I do recall it was very exciting, sitting on those wooden seats and watching the driver change ends when it came to the end of its journey. Once I had a half penny and went to Woolworths and bought a packet of broken biscuits; this was such a treat. I went to a local cricket match on one occasion and each time the bowler came back from a delivery to make his run he stopped and had a swig out of a bottle. I thought it was beer he was drinking as each time he took a drink he would take a wicket. He bowled three men out on the trot. It must have been good beer I thought to myself! We moved back to Gillingham just before I started school and on my first day Mum walked me but after that I took myself. On my way to school I used to pass a greengrocer and I would regularly pinch an apple from the stall outside, probably because I hadn't had any breakfast. In 1937 we moved into a flat over the railway station called West Hall in Kent and the first meal we had was a loaf of bread and a bag of cherries which we ate sitting on the floor. This was a typical example of how Mum was brought up. Eating little food meant I often had a lot of stomach pains when I was a child as I was always so very hungry. Being hungry during my childhood is something I always remember so clearly; there never seemed to be any food in the cupboards. I remember we had very little furniture although we always did have the piano which went everywhere with us. It was Gran's wedding present to Mum and she was really clever at playing the piano even without any music.

Due to moving around so much I wasn't always signed on at school but when I did go, I had a good attendance. A month before Christmas 1938 we ended up moving in with a friend of Mum's whose name was Enid McArdle and her husband was called Jim. They had two children and only had a three-bedroom house so Mum and Dad had to sleep downstairs. Enid had a lodger who was in the army and Pat and I had to sleep in the same bedroom as him. Anyway, this chap, whose nickname was Chippie, woke up one morning and decided to play a trick on Pat. I was already awake and before Chippie put his smelly socks on he told me to keep quiet and then he walked over to Pat's bed. He then waved the socks up and down in front of Pat's nose! "Ha ha," I thought. Pat soon got up and was not amused at all while both Chippie and I were laughing our heads off!

Christmas 1938 and we all went to live with Gran at 71 College Road as Uncle Pat managed to get Dad a permanent job on the council which meant things were better financially. This was all happening while Grandad was still training racehorses in Kent. One day I remember Uncle Pat came home from work on a motorbike and he had a black chow dog in his carrier which he had just bought. Soon after he had the dog he had to go in the army and the dog never saw him for about 5 years. When he finally returned home the dog never reacted at all to begin with just sniffing him. Once the dog realised who it was, he went mad and was all over him not leaving him alone. Pat and me used to go to the local shop and steal sweets. Mum had coupons but no money for us to buy them. Although Pat came with me it was always me who took them but he enjoyed the spoils. How I did this was to ask the shopkeeper to get sweets from the top shelf and take some from the bottom and pass to Pat. One day our Uncle Pat was home on leave and came in the shop as I was doing this. He gave us a good telling off once outside, but this didn't deter us. I have memories of going to the pictures with mum in 1939 when the film Snow White came out and I was really scared.

Also, in 1939, my dad took me to Alexander Park in Epsom and it was while we were there we heard the first air raid warning just after war had been declared with Germany. It was soon after this that Dad went to Guildford to sign up; he was not really the correct age as they took younger men first and Dad was 33. Around this time Grandad returned home as he had a row with the owner at the racing yard. This was because the owner's son, who was assistant trainer to Grandad and learning the ropes wouldn't get out of bed. Grandad being my grandad kicked him out of bed, so that was that. When Dad went for his army training Mum saw a house for rent in West Ewell and we moved there. I remember a jockey with the surname Barber owned it. Grandad had a word with him about a mortgage for Mum which I think he sorted and then lent her the deposit. I'm not too sure about this but I do know that Mum never got any money when Grandad died as she had already had her share. I think that Pat and Ann must have come back home from living with Gran around about this time. I started going up there at weekends probably because I was older now and was more able to keep her company and do some shopping for her. Aunt Noreen was working and living at the hospital and Grandad obviously was no company at all! During that time when the sirens went off for an air raid we would get under the table in the front room or a cupboard under the stairs. When the raids got more intense, we put our bedding in an old pram and pushed it up to Epsom Downs to a big underground shelter built there. We used to walk up after tea and sleep the night there but Grandad being Grandad always stayed at home in bed – bombs or no bombs! When we got fed up with that shelter, we used the underground in Ashley Road which is still there today.

Dad came home on leave about three times before he went abroad and one time he came home when we weren't expecting him. I was out scrumping in a lovely orchard I had found and had my shirt full up with apples and pears and when I saw that he was home I felt sure I was in for trouble. But lo and behold when he saw me, he asked where I got them from. He said that I hadn't got many so he asked me to show him where the orchard was and he took his kit bag with him. I said to Dad that I always walk around the side so no-one sees me but he said we should walk down the middle. I climbed up the tree and threw the fruit to him and he filled his kit bag right up. I thought what a great dad I had who was not frightened of anybody; I felt ten feet tall when I was with him, he was my hero. He always wanted to impress both me and my mum. We had so many pieces of fruit I am sure we never got around to eating them all. Another time when Dad was on leave, I had a fight with a lad and I ended up throwing his jacket in the river. When I got home Dad was there and after a while the local bobby, Sergeant Cleeves arrived and he told Dad what I had done. Dad asked me if this was true and first of all I said no, but he asked me again and I admitted to doing it. I had to get my coat on and Dad told Sergeant Cleeves that he would sort it. This bobby saved me time and time again due to all the trouble I got into, I don't know what would have happened to me without him. Dad walked me the three-mile journey to where this lad lived and made me apologize and then he settled up with his dad for the jacket. When I think about it, I don't know where the money came from but this was always the way Dad punished me, he never hit me. It was around this time he took Ann and I to the pictures and I can remember him buying me a pair of wellington boots.

Whenever Dad was due to return to duty we always knew when his last evening with us would be, but on this particular evening Pat had gone to Gran's and stayed there to go to Epsom Fair so he never got home to see Dad until he was just about to leave. Dad was so upset about this that he lifted him high in the air above his head at the railway station going over the bridge. Mum was so worried that Dad would drop him, which of course he would never do. Sadly, this was the last time we ever saw our dear dad.

I used to make catapults when I was young and I was such a good shot that I would travel around the streets and shoot the milk bottles on the doorsteps; I shouldn't have done this as of course there was a shortage. Sometimes they didn't shatter completely, so I watched the milk just trickle out. Dad taught me how to make the catapult and this was how I did it. I went to the woods and searched for the right prong growing in the branches; a perfect prong is needed to begin with and this could take me ages to find. Once I had that I took it home where I had a spare car tyre collected from the dump which had just the right tension. Then I cut two thin strips each about 7" long and tied one to each prong which would be joined to a piece of leather. I always had a good supply of leather I got from old shoe tongues. This leather would be about 3" long with a slit at each end to thread the rubber through and I then tied it with strong thread. Now I was ready for action! I always had a collection of very small stones as near as I could get them to being round. Of course, marbles were best really, but I needed those for playing with. If it wasn't war time then I would never have done these things as my dad would have been home and I would have been too scared to do anything like that.

In 1940 I was going to school in Ewell High Street and on my birthday, Gran gave me a few marbles and this was a game I became good at so I ended up with quite a collection. I also collected cigarette cards out of bins and I used to play these against the other lads usually winning I might add. We were still so poor that I always wore Pat's cast-off clothing and most of the time I had no soles on my shoes so I used to put cardboard in them. I always had holes in my trousers so Pat refused to walk with me as he was so ashamed of me. I had a few fights especially when I started a new school as I was always the smallest and the bullies picked on me. Once, I saw a lad bullying a smaller lad so I chased him and with my reputation, he ran off. Well, I caught up with him and gave him a good hiding.

I used to play in the park with a crowd of kids and have a game of cricket. We always used the same boy's kit so once he went home his kit went with him and the game was over. I decided to get cocky one day and field in the slips, getting a bit too close to the batsman and ending up with the cricket ball hitting my nose and that is when it got broken; it is still crooked to this day. Another day I went over the park to meet up with my mates and we went on the slide. I went up the slide first and then about five other lads came up behind me so I was supporting them. Of course, being small I couldn't support them for long so I went over the top and got caught up in the bar and broke my leg. The doctor put it in plaster and I had to have six weeks off school. I was always climbing and getting up to mischief. Another time I climbed up a greenhouse in the orchard where I went scrumping and I fell and cut my leg and I still have the scar today. Fortunately, I was with friends at the time so one of them put a tourniquet on it. I never went to the doctor on that occasion but again had to have time off school as I couldn't walk on it.

At school I always used to swing from the water pipes hanging from the ceiling in the toilet. One day my mates were in there so I wanted to show off and I said to them that I would show them how Tarzan swings. With that, I missed the pipe and broke my arm and ended up going to hospital and having it put in plaster and this time it was four weeks off school. That should have taught me not to show off!

One day I came in starving from school as usual and all I could find was a loaf of bread full of mould so I scraped as much off as I could and found a little jam in the bottom of the jar and put that on it and this filled a gap.

I never really attended the church but I did belong to the choir thinking I would get paid, but when pay day came round and I never got anything, I left. Soon after this, I joined the Red Cross and really enjoyed my time there as I was always very proud of my uniform. Towards the end of the war, we had one of the first doodlebugs land in our road. It flattened all the houses on the corner and took all of our doors and windows out. This happened about midnight and mum had to come and get me up as I didn't hear it. When I woke up properly, I thought it had been snowing as all the glass was shattered on my bed, but I was unhurt. Straight away I put on my Red Cross uniform to see if I could help out, but the only thing I remember was a policeman carrying a baby and I never knew whether it was dead or alive. The doodlebug was just like a rocket. It made a terrific noise and just before it crashed down the engine would cut and everyone was waiting for it to land and explode. This happened about 15 seconds after its engine stopped and we used to get these two or three times a day from then on. About six months after the doodlebug, the

V1 rocket was in operation.

This was a missile which could land near enough to where the enemy wanted it to. Fortunately, one never landed near us as these were mostly targeted at cities. Another advanced rocket was also perfected but this never came into operation as it was towards the end of the war. Our protection from these weapons was our Morrison shelter in the living room and our Anderson shelter in the garden leaving our front room locked up so we couldn't mess it up as the 'baby grand' piano was in there.

I remember my brother Pat and I had a 'wood round' and we used to go everywhere canvassing for customers, mainly old people, and once a week we would do our deliveries. We made a cart out of some old pram wheels that we got from the dump and a wooden box and then we nailed two bits of wood on to make the handles. I used to climb over the council fence where they kept plenty of wood and pass it to Pat. We had an old wicker basket that we used to carry the wood in. We charged 3d for half a basket and 6d for a full basket and we cheated with the full basket when wood was hard to come by. We used to stand pieces of wood up in the basket and then lay some wood on top so it looked like it was a full basket. This really wasn't a nice thing to do seeing as they were mainly old people we delivered to. Later on, the council yard used to have the tar blocks so I used to get those as well. When I look back that was probably a wrong move as one of our customers lived in the avenue and unbeknown to us, her husband worked for the council and so he recognized the goods. He told me that he would report me if I did it again. Needless to say, we never delivered to that avenue again, but we still delivered to other roads. All the money I made I used to give to Mum. I'm not sure whether Pat gave Mum his share but I do know we did this for about two years.

Uncle Pat bought both Pat and I a stamp album and he used to send us stamps when he could so we both started collecting them. Because we wanted to get as many as we could we decided to go into Boots (which was where they sold them in those days) and I used to take some without paying! In the end I got very cocky and used to take the albums in with me to check which ones we both wanted. I actually put them in the album while I was there; Pat was always downstairs waiting for me. I did get caught doing this one day as one of the assistants had been watching me and I was halfway down the stairs on the way out when she shouted at me. She asked me what I had in the album and I said nothing and I carried on down the stairs and as soon as I got out of the shop I scarpered. Pat was still waiting outside and didn't know anything about this until I told him when we got home. I remember getting caught scrumping once in Epsom. I went over Epsom College grounds where there was a little orchard and thought I would be able to gather up lots of fruit. I was just on my way out when two men came up to me. "Gotcha!" One of them said they were going to take me to the police station so I had to plead for forgiveness. Fortunately, they didn't take me but told me in no uncertain terms never to do it again (of course I didn't listen and did it again).

When I was eleven, I started at Danetree Road School in West Ewell. Pat was already there and Ann joined us the following year. I remember my PE teacher deciding he would organise boxing training and competitions and I thought that this would be just great for me. In my only fight I was matched with a nice boy just a little bigger than me. I had the time of my life teasing him but not hurting him. After the fight I went into the locker room and there were three boys waiting for me who were all friends of the boy I fought. They told me they didn't like the way I had treated their mate, so I told them that I was just teasing him and not hurting him believing they had no case against me. The boxing never carried on after that and we were never told the reason why. I was really disappointed as I loved nothing better than a good fight, but thinking back there were never any boys as small as me.

Unfortunately, there were no boys' clubs during the war; if there had been I'm sure I wouldn't have got into so much mischief. This being said, I was always brought up to be respectful to my elders, which I always was. I never saw myself as a bad child really and I was well loved at home, it was just that I was always hungry, full of energy and bored. Mum did her best and eventually she did get a full-time job working in the dry cleaners in Epsom doing the alterations. She used to cycle from West Ewell to Epsom on a rickety old bicycle in all weathers. She had to do this as Dad's army pay wasn't a lot and she had the mortgage to pay as well as the bills.

When I reached 12 years old, I was old enough to travel on the trains on my own so I used to skip the train at West Ewell and go nearly as far as London. The reason being that I had started collecting American cigarette cards to play at school and this was the ideal place to find them. These were all from the American troops so were a bit special and only certain American cigarettes had the cards in the packet. The troops used to throw them out in the bins or on the railway lines. I used to get off at the stations on the way and collect what I could, obviously being careful when I went on the lines. I was very good at flicking these cards, and even though I had several friends, I always went on my own as I didn't want to share with anyone.

It was during 1944 nearing the end of the war that Mum received a telegram which she knew meant only one thing. We were playing in the garden and making lots of noise when Mum came out and started screaming at us. We told Mum that we were only playing. She then went on to tell us that our dad had been killed. She ran off to a neighbour somewhere and left us all on our own so I went off crying, away from everyone, sobbing for hours. When I got home, Aunt Noreen was there and she took us all up to Gran's where we stayed for a while. Mum came back after about 3 or 4 days. After this and what with all the bombing, Mum and Gran decided that we would evacuate to Northumberland and we stayed there for about a month, after which we moved to Scotland on the coast and stayed with a relative of Dad's for about 3 months. I loved it there and really enjoyed school. We were situated in a small fishing village called Eyemouth on the east coast of Scotland. The teachers were the best I ever had and I did really well up there, unlike my schooling in England. After a time, we returned to West Ewell and Gran went back to Epsom.

Later that year I decided I wanted to be a jockey so my grandad took me up to a yard in Epsom and put me on a horse using a lunge. This means that the horse is running around in a circle with someone in the middle, which in this case was my grandad, holding onto a long rein. I had never been on a horse before and Grandad chased me around for 15 minutes until I felt sick. Fortunately, it never put me off but reminded me that my grandad was not a very nice man at all.

I used to walk from West Ewell to Epsom Downs after school, having nothing to eat, doing odd jobs at the yard all for no pay. One day after school when I was ready to walk to the stables, Mum came to meet me. She was with a cousin of Grandad's and told me they were going to the pictures and she wanted me to go with them. I said I wanted to go to stables but she said to forget stables for one evening and go with them. I probably had a particularly dirty face on this occasion and it's important to remember my mum was well under 5ft so she had to lean over me to wipe my face. She would spit on her hanky (I can still smell her spit to this day) and wipe my face clean and I don't ever remember being embarrassed about it.

APPRENTICESHIP

After about a month or so of going up to stables I decided that I wanted to leave school. I put this proposal to Mum and she agreed. I was thirteen and a half at the time and the school leaving age was fourteen. When school found out they called me back in and Mum had to go with me. We had to stand before the school board and they were really nasty to Mum about what we did. This was not long after my dad had died and it was so upsetting and I remember my mum crying. I felt that this was such an awful thing to do to my mum. I officially left school in 1945 when I was fourteen years old and went to work for a man my grandad knew at Treadwell House. His name was Mr Charles Bell, a lovely man but not the best man to make a jockey! To this day I have never understood why Grandad didn't put me with the best trainer seeing as he had been in racing all his life but there you go, shows what he thought of me and I was the only one in the family interested in racing. Also, my grandad got me an old pair of 2nd hand breeches which were much too big for me. He also made me wear an old pair of his old-fashioned leather gaiters which came up to my knees. My shoes he also bought 2nd hand that were a size too small for me. Consequently, my feet were all squashed up and my toes remain squashed up to this day!

Again, shows what my grandad thought of me.

I used to go to the pictures at The Capitol in Epsom although I always had to ask someone to take me in. Once in, I would let my mates in who were waiting at the back door. I let them in one by one so that no-one suspected anything. We used to do this regularly and take it in turns to pay; this is what a lot of kids did during the war years.

When I first started work, I used to go back after lunch to clean the tack. I used to have to clean the rusty irons in the sand and this got rid of the rust. Other apprentices from yards next door also did the same and we would meet in the paddock. One day the housekeeper came out of Treadwell House and asked us if we could kill a chicken for her. Well of course we said yes, although not one of us had any idea how to do it. There were three of us lads and I had the first go with no luck, then the other two lads also had a go and again no luck. One of the lads then had an idea. He put his foot on the chicken's head and we all pulled the body and lo and behold the head came off. We stood back in amazement as the chicken got up and ran around and then dropped to the floor. We really didn't know what to tell her but decided to just say that we had cut the head off and bled it. "Well done lads," she said and gave us all 6d each. I used to clean my guvnor's chicken coops out once a week and can remember the cockerel used to always chase and frighten me. The house belonged to Mr Stanley Wootton who also owned nearly all of Epsom Downs although he based himself in Australia at the time where he had a stud farm.

When I started work full-time I used to meet the horses coming in from exercise just off the Downs; this was before they got me a pony to learn to ride on. One day, two horses arrived at the yard and these were both to be trained by Vic Smyth. My guvnor, Mr Bell, looked after some of his horses as he had so many; he had no room for all of them, fact was, he had horses all over the place! Anyhow, these two horses were 3-year-olds, one called Proper Job who was already broken in but the other one called National Spirit wasn't. I remember watching the lads breaking this horse in and this took a few days to do. Anyway, after a couple of days they did manage to get a saddle on, he was a really big raw-boned fellow. While I was watching this day Mr Vic Smyth came along to see how they were getting on and he was a very impatient man when it came to breaking in horses. He was leaning on the paddock gate when he shouted over to our head man called Tim to get on board. I had never seen anything like what I saw next. As I said, he was such a big horse and so very powerful. Talk about 'rodeo'. He bucked so high in the air every piece of tack broke and went flying and poor Tim with it!! Mr Smyth was laughing his head off! When they did manage eventually to break him in he was something special, in fact one of the best horses in the country both flat racing and over the jumps. Little did I realise that one day I would be working for him, if only for a short time. When Mr Smyth's yearlings got off the train in Epsom from the Newmarket sales the lads led them up through the town to the yard on the Downs. From there they didn't put them in stables but took them into the paddock and put the 'breaking tack' on them. Then the lads would ride them around the paddock for about half an hour, all meaning that in one day they had been broken in. I believe that Mr Smyth did this while they were tired from being at the sales all day and the travelling. All trainers used to do things differently but I had never seen this done before and have never seen it done since. It used to take me at least one week to break them in.

While we were at Treadwell House, the police horses were stabled there for the Derby meeting, about ten of them in total. When a policeman saw me looking at them being groomed he asked me if I would like to sit on one. You can imagine how pleased I was, especially when he told me that no-one ever gets on one and told me not say anything about it. This was such an experience for me.

It was around this time we had six German prisoners of war who used to work on Mr Wootton's farm. They would have their meals in the yard cooking their dinner on a gas ring. They used a great big Oxo tin and put all the chopped vegetables in there that they got from the farm. Also, if they managed to catch a rabbit or any game, they used to prepare it and put that in along with the Oxo cubes. Because I watched them, they used to ask me if I would like some, but of course I never did as this was all they had. These soldiers were just very nice, ordinary German lads that were called up during the war.

I started my six-year apprenticeship at 15 and finished at 21. I used to start work at 7am each morning and at first was lodging with Gran and Grandad as it was closer for me. I had the small room downstairs and had no alarm clock but was never late. I came home for lunch at 12.30pm and then went back after lunch to clean the tack and then to stables from 4pm to 6pm and back to Gran's for tea which mostly consisted of bread and jam. When I had been working for three months my guvnor got me a pony to ride which belonged to one of the owners. This pony used to pull his trap and it was built like a little racehorse. I learned to ride on her for a year; Peggy was her name. I found it easy riding Peggy to start with but then when the racehorses left their food and it was given to her, it obviously made her feel really lively and she would leave her box on her hind legs. She used to go through bushes with me and could even keep up with the racehorses when they cantered up the gallops. If we had to wait to get on the cantering ground, what with all the different strings of horses, she used to go flying through all the strings with me and I had no chance of stopping her. Everyone screamed and shouted at me, "Get that bloody pony out of the way!" The good thing was, once I was put on a racehorse after that it wasn't so bad and I had no problems!

After being a whole year on the pony, when I was 15 years-old I was given a grey 3-year-old filly to look after whose name escapes me. When I arrived in the morning at 7am I had to muck her out and put fresh hay and straw in her box and give her water. Then I had to groom her and, being too tiny to put her tack on, one of the paid lads used to do this for me. I rode out on the Downs with the rest of the first lot string for about an hour. When I got back, I could just about manage to take her tack off, but before I did this, I had to make sure I had shut her door because when I took her bridle off, and before I could put the head collar on, she was invariably loose in her box. Being so tiny I couldn't manage to do two things at once. When I had the head collar on, I could tie her to the wall.

First of all, I had to pick her feet out, meaning take all the mud and stones out with a hoof pick and then wash her feet out with a sponge over a bucket of water. Heaven forbids ever letting her feet drop in the water! Then I had to groom her and put her rug on. I was taught always to do the front of the rug first then the girth strap then the second strap that hung under her belly. This one had to be quite loose so when taking the rug off I did this in reverse. Then I could start to get her food ready. This was all prepared for us every day by the head lad. I had to make sure her water was hung in a bucket in the corner and was full up.

When the second string went out, I stayed in the yard and got the hay and straw in all ready for when they got back. When these horses were ready for their food, I also helped to feed them. Going into some of these boxes used to frighten me as they got so excited waiting for their food and started kicking out at me. Now it was lunchtime which meant I went home and then came back to clean the tack before evening stables at 4pm. I had to tie my filly up and start the process again of grooming her. She used to play me up by kicking out at me and frightening me, really taking advantage but when another lad used to come in, she was as good as gold! When this was finished, I put straw litter down to make her comfortable and put the hay net up with the water. After all of this, the head lad would come and look her over and run his hands down her legs to make sure there were no blemishes. It was at that stage I let her loose in her box and my work was done except I had to sweep the yard, finishing at 6pm. This was a typical day at the beginning of my apprenticeship. When this horse left our yard, I was given a 5-year-old little brown gelding with a nickel tube in his neck to help him breath. I had to take this out and clean it every day as it was always full of muck. To do this I had to take the cap off then the side pieces of which there were about four. Then I would wash it out, dry it and put it back. He was a much quieter animal than the filly thank goodness, so no real problems. The idea of the tube was to help his shallow breathing and also when galloping or racing he could run and breathe so much easier. I remember he ran in a race over fences which I didn't take him to and when I got in the following morning he wasn't in his box. I asked where he was and was told he had fallen and broken his back. I was really upset about this as he was a nice, kind little horse. I was then handed a 3-year-old chestnut filly whose name I remember as being

Lombard. She was another nice, no problem horse who gave me a lovely ride.

All this was happening while I lodged with Gran who now and again had her brother Albert to stay. He kept a pub in Hertfordshire and was a nice man. The thing I can't get my head round though is why, when there was a spare room, she always put him in my bed with me and this was a single bed! Probably to save on the washing I have since thought. You can imagine how squashed we both were. I remember he used to put on his night clothes and then take his indigestion medicine and sit on the edge of the bed and start burping. Then he would settle down and push me right up against the wall, so that when I got up in the morning, I used to have to climb all over him.

When I first started work for Charlie Bell as well as doing things in the yard my first job was cleaning the chickens out. There was a ferocious cockerel there and he did frighten the life out of me. When I saw he was out of the way I would make a dash for the coop, something I will never forget. During this time, I had my first ride at Lewes in 1946; this racecourse has been closed for many years now. Grandad came with me representing Mr Charlie Bell and walked the course with me in the morning. He told me what to do at certain times during the race and I always replied, "Okay Grandad." He got really cross with me for saying that and said, "Never say that, say very well," when you respond. Being just 5 stone, I couldn't carry the weight cloth as well as the saddle, so Grandad carried the weight cloth for me. Well, I did quite well as I was only beaten a short head for 2nd place but I thought I was just second but no photo finishes in those days. The lad who beat me was also having his first ride and he turned out to be a good apprentice. Coming down the hill it was the fastest I had been in my life. In total I had three rides in 1946 and eight rides in 1947. In racing, it has always been a rule that respect is paramount. Touching your cap, speak when spoken to and always say 'sir' or 'madam'. No problem for me with my upbringing as it was second nature.

A man named Peddler Warwick was my valet and, depending on the meetings, I had him several times as he did all of Mr Wootton's jockeys so therefore I was in good company. Anyway, the first time he made me ready he gave me ladies stockings to put on under my boots and breeches; I never realised this is what happened and would you believe all the stockings were laddered.

In 1948 I had my first ride on Chwarau Teg, which is Welsh and means Fair Play. This ride was at Royal Ascot and I had never even sat on him before and we finished nowhere! One week later on June 25th, I rode him a winner at Doncaster. One of Mr Bell's head lads walked the course with me and told me exactly where to make my run, which was about a furlong out, and I won by 2 lengths. Thus began a winning association with the best horse I have ever ridden in a race. When I left the racecourse with Gordon Greathurst, another jockey of my age, there were about five young girls waiting for my autograph! "Am I famous?" I thought. I often wonder what happened to those girls and do they still have my autograph? When I got back to Gran's and told everyone I had ridden my first winner the only thing my grandad said to me was, "You have ridden a winner now you forget about it." Gran, of course, was different and said, "Well done Tony". She told me to go to the off-license, as the owner Jack Stanton promised me any drink I wanted once I had ridden a winner. She told me to ask for a bottle of brandy. I did as Gran asked but when I arrived at the off-license Jack told me I wasn't old enough to purchase spirits! I used that shop a lot for Gran buying her cigarettes and Guinness. Anyway, after that first winner he never bothered with me as he was probably scared that when I got older he would have to give me the bottle of brandy!

All the racing lads used to go down the town to the café on

the corner of Pound Lane where the old music hall used to be for a cup of tea. I used to go and join them after I had been swimming and before going back to stables. There was another apprentice who also worked for Mr Bell and his name was Roy Bray. I used to go to his home for an hour in the evening, he was a very friendly lad and I remember him well. One of his sisters was married to Freddie Laker the owner of an airline company that was very popular then, and the other sister was married to a jockey called Billy Hollick. Roy also had a good-looking sister who was still at school and we used to play kiss chase on Epsom Common; I used to chase her and she let me catch her! She used to do dancing at school and one Christmas was in a pantomime at Wolverhampton and she sent me a photo of her dressed up. Gran and Aunt Noreen used to open my mail so they saw this photo before I did. They wrote to this girl and told her that I was not interested in girls only interested in my career and telling her never to get in touch again! This was very embarrassing for me as you can imagine but their views were very Victorian.

My brother Pat used to come up some Sunday evenings and we used to go the pictures at The Odeon in Epsom. I used to have to ask for the tickets though, due to Pat's stutter, and he had to stand behind me as I wasn't old enough to get in.

Early in my second year of my apprenticeship my filly that I looked after called Lombard was hired out to a film company who were making a film called 'Esther Waters' and this came out in 1948. It was a British period drama and was to include racing scenes which were filmed on Epsom racecourse. There were quite a few horses in it from different stables. They dressed me up in old fashioned clothes that were worn by horse grooms 100 years previous. This filming went on for a week and my pay was 30 shillings a day! I saw this film many years later but there were no racing scenes in it, so they must have been cut out by the time the film came out. So, my few scenes as an 'actor' were thwarted but I did earn a good few quid. Mind you I never got my 30 shillings a week wages from my guvnor!

Another thing I was pleased about, once I had ridden my first winner, was I never had to go back early to clean the tack. Shortly after I rode my first winner, I rode the same horse in a race at Kempton Park. He was 2nd favourite and had a very good chance of winning in a field of 4 runners. The three other jockeys were Tommy Weston, Charlie Smirk and Kenny Gethin. When we got down to the starting gate no one spoke to me as I was only an apprentice. They had already decided what they were going to do as they had all worked out who was going to win and had placed money on it, also working out where I would be. My orders from my guvnor were to sit 2nd or 3rd and to keep my eye on the favourite which was Wild Rebel ridden by Tommy. As soon as we jumped off, I went to move into 3rd place and Kenny Gethin came across me and boxed me against the rail and said, "Stay there you little bastard." I remained boxed in until 2 furlongs out when he said to me, "Time to go now son," and he let me out! By then, Wild Rebel was five or six lengths in front. I made up a lot of ground and was only beaten by half a length. I was too nervous to mention it to my guvnor as was the same with most apprentices in those days being just after the war when all the jockeys were coming back. If they could stop an apprentice riding a winner then they would. Of course, this would never go on nowadays with all the cameras around.

In the last year of the war, Uncle Pat was in Italy at one end and Dad at the other. They always said that they would meet up, but with Dad being killed, that never happened. Uncle Pat brought me back a German dagger which I put in my room at Gran's, however, somehow it went missing and it was never found by me. Harry, a cousin of Grandads who came from Manchester came to visit and gave me a gold fishing medal he had won; again, this went missing. Many years later we went to see Aunt Noreen and she brought it out to show us. I told her it was mine and she said she thought Harry had given it to her, anyway, then she did give it back. What with the episode of opening my mail and these two items 'going missing' all goes to show that in those days the older generation would take responsibility for the younger generation away from them.

Gran and Grandad had a radio in the living room and Grandad always used to listen to the news at 6pm then he would turn it off and go to bed. Once he had gone up, I would ask Gran if I could listen to Dick Barton at 6.45 and of course, she agreed. One day Grandad turned the radio off but was hanging about and Dick Barton had started so I started making signs to Gran to turn it on before he left the room. That was a bad move as she turned it on and Grandad went mad with me and told me to pack my bags and go home. Gran said, "If he goes, I go," thinking he would change his mind but he said, "Well, you go as well then." I went back to Mum at West Ewell and of course Gran stayed with Grandad.

Twice in 1947 I used to get on the Green Line bus in

Epsom and travel to Dunstable to ride work for a racehorse trainer called Mr Bunker who trained in a little village called Bray near Leyton Buzzard. I had a couple of rides for him and used to stay, along with the head lad, in digs they had found for us. He was a big pig farmer and very rich, but I never got to see any of his money. While I was there and riding out one day, I saw a stoat get hold of a rabbit in a field and kill it.

The same year a young lad called John Carter came to work for Mr Charlie Bell, but in a different yard and we became very good friends. John sadly passed away in 1995; we were very close. John came over from France in 1946. His mum was French and they were living there with relatives when war broke out. Because he spoke fluent French, he was asked to join the French Resistance which he declined but did agree to deliver messages on his bike for them. In 1944 he tried to escape from France and got as far as the Pyrenees and it was there that he got a job with a man who owned a horse, so he stayed there, hence his love of horses.

In the same year I went to ride work for Mr Tim Bell (my guvnor's brother) for a couple of weeks. He also trained in Bray and the yard was in a big farm which belonged to a lovely couple, Mr and Mrs Mitchell. Mr Mitchell had been a speedway rider and had a bad accident which left him a little brain damaged, therefore he was a very quiet man. It was a cattle farm and he had a yard built with 20 boxes. They had about 8 horses of their own; the rest belonged to other owners. I used to ride out 2 lots for him and lived with the owners in a big house; the other lads lived in the village. After riding out, if Mr Mitchell was going out shooting rabbits, I would go with him. As well as shooting them he used to put his hand down the little bolt holes and often would pull out a rabbit that had been hiding in there. Also, very often Mrs Mitchell would take me into the barns looking for wild cats breeding inbetween their bales of hay. She would destroy the babies if she could catch them! I did have a couple of rides for them but their horses weren't much good.

I went to Birmingham for a ride towards the end of the season of 1947 and stayed overnight. I thought I would go to the theatre as the pantomime was just starting. I remember it must have been Cinderella as Norman Wisdom was in it and he was Buttons. Norman had not been long out of the forces so he was not really well known, but he did make the show and had a great future ahead of him as we all know.

When it was known that Mr Charlie Bell was moving to Upavon in Wiltshire it was arranged that I would have my indentures transferred to either Mr Harold Wallington or Mr Peter Thrale. Two weeks before he was due to leave my guvnor said he wanted to take me with him. I really wasn't bothered either way because I rode a winner two weeks before and wherever my grandad put me 'they didn't make jockeys'. Because of this, no-one ever taught me how to race ride so what I had to do was watch and learn.

Therefore, in the summer of 1948 I found myself living in a little village in Wiltshire, a very backward village with a population of about 1000 surrounded by other small villages around Salisbury Plain where the main occupation was farm work, although a lot of the people worked at the air force camp or for the local rabbit catcher. As you can imagine, this was an alien way of life to me having always lived in towns. Most of the properties had no electric, no water and no sanitation, just a well in the garden. The journey there in a horsebox seemed to take forever. The yard Mr Charlie Bell had was called 'Grey Flags' and it had room for twenty horses; we took fifteen with us. This yard was owned by Lord Eliot who we called 'Lordy' and his large house was also called 'Grey Flags' where he lived with his wife. Lordy had an army jeep and he took me and the paid lads around different digs to see where we could all lodge. In those days, times being hard, so many people took lodgers in to supplement their wages. I stayed with an Irish lad called Paddy with a lady called Mrs Stevens. Paddy was twenty-four at the time and came from a good family in Ireland. This lady was near enough 6ft tall and a widow of about 50 years old with just one son at home; Paddy and I shared a room. She also had a sister in the village where another older lad lodged, and he was the lucky one as she lived in one of the new council houses built up on the hill just outside the village which had all the mod cons! Mrs Stevens was very regimental, meals on time etc. and the food was very basic. Of an evening, after tea, we would go to the next village called Rushall and play cricket with the village lads. One evening we got home about 9pm and she was stood at the door waiting for us and said, "Where have you been? Your supper is on the table getting cold." Would you believe supper consisted of a lettuce leaf and a tomato! When we got to our room Paddy told me he had enough of this and would sort somewhere else to lodge and I agreed with him.

Every morning, after exercising the horses, we used to go the village café, which was also the local telephone exchange. This was run by Sylvia and Joe Richardson, a lovely couple. Sylvia was a very good-looking girl about twenty-two years old and Joe was about five years older.

Unbeknown to me, Paddy had already arranged with Sylvia that she would take us in as lodgers. Well, these were fantastic digs and I even learnt to operate the telephone exchange. One afternoon when I came back Paddy was up in the bedroom and he said to me, "Guess what's just happened? Sylvia has just been in our bedroom making advances to me!" Of course, I was shocked but on looking back, I think maybe he had been chatting her up when he used to go to the café and this is why she wanted us as lodgers! So, the relationship had progressed from then and of course when Joe found out we had to go, having only been there about two weeks.

We quickly found fresh digs, this time with a lady called Mrs Duckett who only had one leg and used to go up and down the stairs on her bottom. No mod cons there but all we did was sleep there as we had all our meals with the lovely Mrs Ayres. We were lucky in the fact that we were getting good food and things rolled along for about three weeks. But then all changed as Mrs Duckett used to go and visit her old lodger called Doc in a mental home in Devizes. When he was discharged he came back and lived with her and slept in our bedroom would you believe? I was okay with this. As long as Paddy was there with me I felt safe, but one time when Doc came back Mrs Duckett turned into a right witch so yet again Paddy came home and said he had enough of this 'old cow' and was leaving. Of course, I wanted to leave too, but Paddy said I shouldn't as the guvnor wouldn't like it if we both kept leaving our digs. Paddy was okay as he had already got fixed up with Mrs Ayres but I had to stay, which was hell as I was still only 17 and so immature and tiny for my age. Then to cap it all, one evening Mr Bell said to me that Mrs Duckett had been to see him to tell him that I had been coming home drunk from the pub and saying nasty things. I was flabbergasted as I never went to the pub and certainly never drank and was always very respectful, so I told Mr Bell that all this was untrue. He told me that he knew that but advised me to get out as soon as Mrs Ayres had a room available. I did have this out with Mrs Duckett, not that it did much good. I had to stay for a few more weeks being scared out of my life sleeping in the same room as Doc.

While I was still with the witch, I had a chance of a ride but had to lose weight in order to do this. This was in the summer and John Carter took me for a long run, about 8 miles while he rode his bicycle. He made me put on lots of jumpers and he also took an overcoat on his bike. After I had run about 5 miles, he put the coat on me and when we got back home, he took me up to the bedroom and put me in bed with all the clothes still on and sat on me! He wouldn't let me get up and I really thought I was going to die. I had to fight him to get him off me and when I got out of bed, I was dripping wet, but as least I lost 7lbs! I will never forget this as I thought I was suffocating. All I had that night to eat was a thin slice of bread with jam sparingly spread. When I got weighed it was at the local butchers and he said to me, "Can I have a bet on this horse?" I told him not to bother as it was a donkey! He asked me why I was losing all this weight. "Why? For £7 of course," I said!

While all this was going on, Mrs Ayres' dad was ill with cancer. They lived in the High Street so when he died, she moved in with her mum and because it was a bigger house this enabled me to go and lodge there. Paddy had moved out by this time, but I was in heaven as these were the best digs ever! I remained friends with this lovely lady right up to when she died at the age of 99. Once I managed to settle down in the village with the right lodgings, life started to look good. Mr Bell and his wife Dorothy lived in the cottage nearby. Lord Eliot made a gym out of the saddle room for me to do my boxing. I was the only apprentice there and there was never any mention of a boxing trainer for me. Sometimes some of the village lads used to come and spar with me but they were useless. There was no means of transport so the boxing fizzled out for me seeing as I had no trainer and no one to spar with. Why I never thought to catch the local bus to Devizes and join their local boxing club I will never know. After that I used to go to the cinema at the air force camp, either by bus or on foot, sometimes the local village lads went with me. By this time, I was showing an interest in the local girls, but being in a tiny village everyone knew each other's business.

We had been in Upavon for six weeks and another head lad had to be found and we were lucky to engage a lovely man called Darkie Nichols. Previously, he had worked on the gas but had worked for Mr Stanley Wootton in the past and Mr Bell knew him from years gone by as he was well into his 50's. He came to visit Mr Bell with his wife and two girls and Mr Bell must have spun him a yarn as he encouraged him to be head lad. He used to clip the jumpers in the winter, and my being the only apprentice at the time, I used to go back in the afternoons to help out. There wasn't much Darkie didn't know about horses and he was very good to me. The clipping machine in those days was manual and I had to turn the handle while he clipped the horse; he would manage to get one done in an afternoon. This machine was similar to a meat mincer but of course far bigger and it was hard work keep turning the handle.

Also, if the horse wouldn't stand still, I would have to tie one of its front legs up. While Darkie was clipping, he would sing all the time. As he used to go round the local pubs of an evening singing for pleasure, maybe he got a couple of drinks out of it. Anyway, the song he always sang while clipping was 'That Lucky Old Sun' and by the time he had clipped all of the horses I also knew all of the words and still remember them today. He took a real liking to me and he asked me to his home some weekends for dinner and tea. His two lovely daughters were around my age called Maureen and Babs. Some Friday evenings he and his family would pick me up and we would go for a pub crawl around Beckhampton where all the racing lads would be having a drink. Darkie, having such a good voice, would get them all to have a sing song; not me though as if I had sung, I was frightened they would all walk out! I was not a drinker in those days but would have a shandy.

His youngest daughter Maureen ran a dance school in Devizes teaching children ballet and grown-ups ballroom dancing. After stables, I would go round once or twice a week and she would give me private tuition for free. She taught me all the basic steps for the ballroom. Well, one day when riding out I said to Darkie, "What do you think if I asked Maureen to go out with me?" His reply was most adamant that she was not interested in courting. I knew by the tone of his voice he never wanted me to ask her. Anyway, not many months after she met a racing lad with a wonderful voice and took a fancy to him and started courting him. Darkie was very possessive of his family calling them 'his gang' and he didn't want anyone breaking the foursome up. This racing lad really made good and, in the end, had his own garage in Bristol and they got married and Maureen did very well for herself having two show horses for her two children and a big house with a paddock. Babs also got married not long after so the gang did get broken up!

While working with Darkie, I did ride the horse he looked after a winner. It was usual in those days to give the lad a drink for that. I said to him, "You can have £5 now or wait for Christmas and have £10." Darkie said he would wait for the £10 and when Christmas came, he asked for his money. I told him I wasn't going to give him the money on principle as he was being greedy!! He laughed his head off as we were such good mates. Years later we did have a Christmas card from 'The Greedy Lad' and this took me some time to work out who it was from but when I did, we decided to go and catch up with him. We found where he was living and I knocked on his door. At first, he didn't know who I was but took me indoors to see his wife and she knew me straight away. They were thrilled to see me again. When Darkie was with Mr Stanley Wootton, he was about twenty-four years old and after stables, Mr Wootton used to put a ring up in the saddle room to train apprentices how to box. One time, Darkie was sparring with a big apprentice and being a bit hard on him so Mr Wootton stopped it, told the apprentice to get out of the ring but for Darkie to stay. Mr Wootton then put on boxing gloves and got in the ring and proceeded to give Darkie a boxing lesson never sparing any of the punches! In fact, Darkie said to me afterwards that he really hurt him. While working for Mr Bell Darkie went racing with the horse that I rode the winner on and he met up with Mr Wootton. He went up to him and said, "Hello sir, I bet you don't know who I am?" to which he replied, "Oh yes I do Darkie." Darkie said to him, "A bit different nowadays to old days is it not sir, when you used to look around the yard inspecting the horses and wearing white gloves?" These were put on to feel over the horse for signs it hadn't been groomed properly!! Mr Wootton agreed but also said, "But do you remember I used to look around also carrying a big stick." At this Darkie laughed as of course he remembered that!

The village folk liked and respected me. They thought I was wonderful with my name in the daily papers nearly every day! The girls also thought I was special being a 'Townie'.

I had many rides in the year of 1948, but sometimes found it rather stressful getting to and from the different meetings. Anyhow, by the end of the season of 1948 I finished quite well with nearly 100 rides under my belt.

I went to The Bear pub in Devizes one evening with some of the lads. A Salvation Army Girl came in, very good looking she was, she was selling their magazine but all the lads said they wouldn't buy one until she got up and sang for us which she duly did. We all decided to buy a magazine from her so she did well out of it. There were 2 pubs in Upavon called The Ship and The Antelope and both of the publicans had young daughters. One of the daughters I took out for about a month and the other one I just used to chat up! There were so many girls in the village I must have taken out about 6 of them and then there were girls in the other villages I took out also. I had the time of my life!

Here's a little story concerning an outside ride for a Midland trainer by the name of Mr Langley, a very nice man who trained a few horses near Worcester. He rang up my guvnor to ask if I could ride a horse called Fairborn

Gorse which was to run at Birmingham (a 7- furlong race) on 3rd May 1948 (coincidentally my sister Ann's 16th birthday). I forget if he said anything to me about the horse or how he wanted him ridden. When the lad was leading him out from the paddock to the racecourse, he told me to be careful as he was a very strong horse and a strong puller – meaning he tries to run away with you. Well, I don't know how I even managed him going down to the start! When we got in our draw position and walked in, he took off with me and went straight through the starting gate; how I pulled him up I will never know. When I lined up at the start a second time I stood with his back to the gate and when the rest of the field walked to the start, I turned him around to jump off with the rest of them. My goodness was he fast? He made all the running for 6½ furlongs and I thought I was surely going to win. He then began to fade and started to tire and the first to pass me was Gordon Richards and, in the end, I finished 4th. A few weeks later I saw this horse was running in a race at Worcester with another apprentice riding him. I thought to myself, well good luck because you're gonna need it! I had a ride the next day at Worcester so when I bumped into the trainer, I enquired how his horse had run. He told me that he wished I had been there as, apparently, the horse had run away with the boy and jumped the railings and the boy ended up in hospital. He was in there for ten weeks! I wouldn't wish the boy any bad luck, but I did wonder why he never asked me to ride the horse. The next time this horse ran it was at Worcester again and he asked me if I would ride it which I did. It was 7 furlongs again and this time we got down to the start and he got excited just like before. He ended up getting tangled up in the starting gate, so this had to be taken down and untangled. The horse was hung up by one of the thick rubber strands that make up the starting gate and it got tangled around his jaw and the horse was on the floor. This was sorted and we made all the running again, but same as before, he faded at the last ½ furlong. He was 4th again and that was the last I heard of him. Looking back, I do think they may have given him something to help him run like that!

We had a 2-year-old filly in the yard called 'Neat & Shady'. She came down from Mr Johnny Dines in Epsom; my grandad got a lift in the horsebox. He came to tell me that Gran said for me to give him my money from my bank so that she could put it in my post office book. That only left me with a little bit of pocket money, but that is what it was like in those days, you did as you were told. Anyway, Mr Dines said to Mr Bell, "If you win a race with this filly, I will give you £100," a lot of money in those days. She was entered in a selling race at Thirsk and Mr Bell thought she would win. A selling race means after the race the winner comes up for sale and in my day, what happened was, if you were a real gentleman and wanted to bid for it, you used to ask the trainer if he wanted to keep the horse. Then if he said no and there were two or three people bidding for it, this made the price higher. This was then a knock-on effect for the second horse as the higher the price meant the second horse got a higher percentage. The lad who looked after her came with us from Epsom and he was an old jockey by the name of Titch Grantham. She never felt to me as though she was going to win and, in the end, I finished in the middle of a big field of runners.

I really enjoyed going to Thirsk to ride as the digs were so good and they really made a fuss of me. They used to take Titch and me down to their social club of an evening. The older women used to sit me on their laps. I was so tiny and well-mannered and they loved that!

In July 1948 I was in the weighing room at Hurst Park changing to ride in one of the races. One of the racecourse officials came in and asked me if I could spare a moment as my mum was outside wanting to talk to me. Charlie Smirk had the same valet as me and he was also changing so he overhead all this. He said to me, "Go on sonny, go and see what mummy wants, don't keep her waiting!" On hearing that, Pedlar our valet said to him, "Come on Charlie, you can stop that, I remember when your mummy and daddy came to see you with a fruit and vegetable barrow outside!" With that, 'The Big Chief of the Weighing Room' said no more! So away I went to see Mum who had been let in by Sergeant Cleeves who had now retired and was security on the gate. This was a good chance for Mum and me to meet up seeing as I was living in Upavon and such a great surprise for me. She never did let on as to whether she had a few pennies on my horse; I do hope not though as it was 4th.

The next time 'Neat & Shady' ran was at the end of the year at Wolverhampton and she wasn't fancied. Mr Bell told me to have a good ride and finish as near as I could to the winner. There were a lot of runners, two lines of them in fact. Down at the starting gate I thought to myself that I really wanted this filly to run well as the owner was a lovely man. I was getting a little excited about it at the start and didn't want to be away slowly. Gordon Richards (who was riding in this race also) said to me, "Don't worry son, walk in with me." Well, I knew the starter wouldn't let the gate go up unless Gordon was there and ready so I was fine. I jumped off well and took the lead at the distance and won half a length. I was amazed when walking back in as Titch met me and was so excited he nearly pulled me off. He had all his savings on her to win and the price was 25-1. Consequently, he went back to Epsom a very happy man. The next year when I went back to Thirsk and stayed in the same digs, they all started kissing me and telling me what a wonderful boy I was. That was because they all backed 'Neat & Shady' and won a lot of money. Titch had told them not to back her when she ran at Thirsk but to wait until she ran at Wolverhampton. This is so mind boggling to me and I asked myself, "What happened to her at Thirsk?" Anyway, 1948 finished well and we always had a good Christmas in the village.

Once again, I rode another horse for a small trainer called Langley at Wolverhampton in the last race of the day. His orders were, "She's not up to this class of race." It was one and a half miles, with just 4 runners and the other 3 were very good, top-class horses. "But," he said, "Make a show and make the running for as far as you can." Well, all apprentices would love these great orders where you can kick on in front and I was no exception! So, we got down to the starting gate and walked in to jump off and believe it or not that is the last I saw of the 3 horses! By the time I was passing the grandstand the bookmakers were packing up to go home, but they did all turn around and clap me! When I returned to the paddock the first three horses had left the enclosures even! Such an embarrassment to me and I forget what I said to the trainer when I got off. The only thing I remember I said was, "Have I missed my train home?" No reply to that question though, but I got my 7 guineas riding fee.

Another day I went to Birmingham to ride a horse for another trainer; well, this horse was rubbish which I told the trainer when I finished. He said, "Well I want you to tell the owner that." When he introduced the owner to me it was an elderly lady in a wheelchair. I told her that her horse was a good ride but thought she would never win a race!

Off I went to Chepstow another day to ride a horse called 'Panara' for a small trainer in a 5-furlong sprint. My weight was 6 stone 7lb including the saddle and there were 10 good animals in this race. The trainer told me how he wanted me to ride her and would you believe I was 2nd. I lead from 2 furlongs out and Gordon Richards rode the favourite which wasn't in the first 3! But I realised then that the other horses weren't trying that day so I was 2nd to a very good horse called 'Your Fancy'. When I got in, I thought the trainer was going to kiss me as he told me he had never seen her run like that before! He asked me to ride the same horse at Haydock and I asked my guvnor and he said yes. This time the horse had 10 stone on its back and my weight was 6st 7lb at the time so the clerk of scales said to the trainer, "Do you want this boy to ride this horse with all this dead weight?" "I certainly do!" was the reply. Thank goodness the horse ran well and although not in the first three, she gave me a good ride finishing fourth.

I seem to remember the severe winter of 1948-49 which was quite normal on Salisbury Plain what with there being no shelter. I was in such good digs and life was so much better for me as for a start, I didn't need to go out every evening and this suited me very well. Weekends were always welcome as there was a village dance with all the young girls sitting around waiting for someone to partner them although there were only a handful of 'lookers'.

Lady Eliot was a very attractive woman and every year she would borrow the stable hack, which the trainer used to ride to go on the Downs to follow the horses. She would get the lads to spruce the hack up like he was going to a show. Then she would bring her side saddle out to be put on and then go and change into her long black skirt, black top hat with a veil, black gloves and black jacket. She was now ready to attend the local foxhound meet. This has always stayed with me because for a woman of her age, she always looked so elegant and classy.

In the yard we had a little black cat to keep the vermin down who survived on just one saucer of milk each day when we had our tea. Every morning there were always one or two rats lying around half eaten. This cat even used to jump in the river and bring water voles out. He used to sleep on the back of one of the horses we had in the yard during the day and would you believe this horse was very bad tempered but never bothered about the cat.

When the flat season started that year, I was a lot heavier around about 7st 3lbs but this didn't stop me getting a good few rides early on. I even managed to ride a winner at Bath. I was also getting a number of outside rides for different trainers and although these were not particularly good horses, they did help boost my bank balance.

I used to swim in the river Avon and I was very content with my life what with the sun shining and the young girls looking great in their summer dresses. We used to have one of the biggest carnivals in the West Country, held in a village near to Upavon called Pewsey. It used to last about two hours and was such a sight not to be missed. When the fair came to town that year, I happened to meet a very nice young girl there. She went to Marlborough Grammar School which was the same school that Mrs Ayres' son Peter went to. We managed to see each other for about six weeks with Peter delivering our messages; it was all good while it lasted!

1949 arrived and being 18, I was conscripted for army service but with Mr Bell's authorisation was granted a year's deferment due to my apprenticeship. The same thing happened in 1950 and I got deferred again as you were allowed a maximum of two years to defer.

During the post war years there were quite a few racecourses that opened up for the first time after being closed for the duration and one of these was Warwick. On its first day of racing I had five rides; the racecourse wasn't in very good condition as the bends proved to be very slippery. My ride in the first was on the filly 'Neat & Shady' and we slipped up on the bend into the straight. I was taken to the medical room as I hurt my backside; I still have the scar to prove it. I had a ride in the second race and the owner was very concerned about me as this 2-year-old was a horse they really fancied to win. I satisfied him that I was fine although I wished afterwards that I hadn't as I got left at the starting gate and only finished fourth. This was a huge let down but on looking back the horse did have a deformed neck which caused his head to be all screwed to one side making him a horrible ride. I also remember the ride I had in the last race; it was on a 3 year old filly from our yard called 'Hooray'. While we were walking around at the start it was raining very hard with thunder and lightning. There were only four runners in this race and Sir Gordon Richards was on board one of the runners. His words to us all were, "Now let's take it nice and steady as there have been enough accidents today." We all agreed to this and started slowly, then when entering the straight Doug Smith kicked his horse on aiming to slip the field. He never got around the bend, he slipped up and we galloped all over him! Gordon gave him a right good telling off for that when we got back to the weighing room. This was a bad day for me, slipped up in the first and got left in the second and a terrible storm in the last. I had a total of five rides and not one of them in the first three.

Wolverhampton had the same problem with the bends. I had three rides there when it first opened and in one of the races I rode in there were about fifteen runners over a mile and a quarter. What a shambles it was as four horses came down; I saw Charlie Smirk fall in front of me. The animal got up but Charlie was hung up in the stirrup iron but being the man he was, he managed to get his hands to the reins and pull the horse up and get his foot out. What an incredible jockey he was.

Mr Bell had a couple of horses obtained from Belgium with one of them finishing second in the Belgium Derby. This horse was a real tyke and didn't enjoy life or racing. When you asked him to go he wouldn't and if you didn't want him to go, he would! On one occasion I rode him at Pontefract and there were five runners in a pretty good race. Mr Bell said, "Don't be in the first three, just see how good he is." Coming into the straight I was third and going easy, or so I thought. The leader and second were 5 lengths in front and I didn't want to finish third. Davy Jones, who was one of the more experienced jockeys of the time, was sitting on my quarters and he also didn't want to finish in the first three. He looked over to me and shouted out, "Kick on son," but I took no notice so he pulled his whip through and started hitting my horse across his quarters. My horse, being the tyke he was, started to slow down. Consequently, Davy Jones finished third and I was fourth. Pulling up Davey said to me, "What is wrong with you son, you could have got third." His face was a picture when I said, "I didn't want to finish in the first three." Both Davy Jones and my horse were saving their best for another day and didn't want to be exposed. When we got into the weighing room there was hell to pay when I told Mr Bell.

As the season progressed, I found that I was putting on weight and in those days, trainers were always after young apprentices to claim the riding allowance and if you couldn't claim it then you probably didn't get the rides. When jockeys were called out into the paddock if Gordon Richards was riding, I used to follow him, walking the same as he did! If it was cold and he had his overcoat on I would go and put mine on as well. Silly things really, but that is what I did. I also used to watch him and the other jockeys riding to see how to do it properly.

One day, after finishing morning stable, my guvnor came and said to me, "Hang on a minute Tony, I want you to wait here until the man comes to put that horse down in the corner box. When he arrives can you put the bridle on and take him to the paddock for the chap?" I did all this and once he arrived, I had to hold the horse steady. The instrument he used to do the deed was shaped like a bell and was very old fashioned. He held it against the horse's forehead with one hand and struck the handle of the bell with a hammer. I had to stand well back whilst still holding the horse because the horse went down so quickly, like a ton of bricks. This was not a job I relished at all. The next time I did this was when I came out of the army and had to hold a horse called 'Solid Man' while he was shot. He had such bad legs and this was a horse I had ridden over fences. He was owned by the late racing commentator Peter O'Sullivan. For me, this was the darker side of racing yet this is what is called a 'humane killing' as the horse didn't know anything and didn't suffer. What got to me was that the horses that end up like this didn't get a chance to finish their life out in the field.

Lord Eliot was always backwards and forwards to his club in London where he stayed while in town. One day when he returned, he told us to gather around in the saddle room and said, "I have a joke to tell you." He was always telling us his funny jokes he got from his club. But this particular one I remember well. "There was this chap who had a parrot which performed tricks in pubs and clubs. Well, the parrot was walking a tightrope doing a balancing act and the audience were laughing their heads off. So, he turned round and said to the audience, ludicrous no doubt but f****** difficult!" Lord Eliot was always able to tell a joke and made you laugh even if it wasn't that funny! He was a big man about 6ft 4in tall with a handlebar moustache. My dear friend, John Carter, asked Lord Eliot if he could play football to which he replied, "Play football, of course I can, I'm a good goalkeeper!" John asked if he would play in goal for Upavon and he said he would be only too pleased to help out. We soon discovered that he wasn't joking he really was a good goalie. Mind you, being 6ft 4in tall and an ex-guardsman did help! Also, he was always up for anything.

One Sunday during that season after I had eaten my dinner, I was just taking my towel down to the river for a swim when I bumped into the guvnor's daughter. She told me that Mr Bell wanted to see me. He told me that I had two rides at Birmingham the following day; these were for a trainer I had never heard of. I had to go and catch a bus to Marlborough, then another one to Swindon and then the train to Birmingham. When I finally got there, I had to find a place to stay. All this travel for two rides meaning I was missing my swimming in the river with all the local girls! The irony is that both of the animals finished last, one of the horse's names being 'Ann's Choice'.

I really did enjoy my life so much in the country, never thinking about going home. Mind you, I don't think my guvnor would have spared me even if I had wanted to. I always made sure I rang Mum every two weeks and I still remember our number to this day; 1698. I finished that season reasonably well totalling 60 rides and managed to get home for a week once the season had finished. I was always so pleased to go and visit my gran although when she saw me, she would pull me aside and ask me to settle the money that Mum had owed her. She used to say that I was in a position of responsibility and I never minded really as I did feel it was my duty.

On returning to Upavon for Christmas and entering a new decade another hard winter riding out on the gallops lay ahead. It was so cold! By the time the flat season arrived I was over a stone heavier. Starting the season at 8st 3lb I managed to get down to 7st 12lb. I ended up just having twenty or so rides that year. At the end of that season we had another cold winter ahead of us spent riding out our jumpers. One morning Mr Bell asked me if I would like to ride a horse owned by Peter O'Sullivan called 'Solid Man' in a chase at Wolverhampton before I went in the army. I had ridden him out many times so I knew what he was like and that he would be a great ride, so of course I said yes. Mr Bell was pleased and asked me to pop him over three fences on our way back to the yard. There were two plain fences and an open ditch. This was such a thrill for me as I had never been on a horse over fences before. He took the fences really well as he was such a good jumper and very safe to ride. On the day of the race the on-course bookmakers made him favourite (probably due to the name of Anthony Bowles riding him!) Unfortunately, he never finished in the first three but I did come back safe. I was well satisfied having my first ride over jumps and could go into the army reasonably happy. After having a ride over national hunt this meant that if I had a ride on the flat again, I wouldn't be able to claim my apprentice allowance as this was transferred to jumping.

In February 1951 I started my two years conscription. Lord Eliot called me into the saddle room and said he wanted to give me some important advice. He told me never to volunteer for anything and asked me once I was settled in to let him know how I was doing and he would keep in touch. He was a man of his word as both he and Lady Eliot frequently sent me letters to which I always replied. I still have those letters to this day. Unfortunately, I never managed to attend his club but they did make arrangements to meet me in White City. However, something their end happened and they never made it. They were divorced in 1959 when Lord Eliot became the 9th Earl of St Germans in Cornwall after his father died. After this he spent all of his time on his yacht and I never saw or heard from him again. The same went for Lady Eliot, who was in fact Lord Eliot's second wife. She did live in London for a time and then re-married. The marriage was not a happy one as her husband only married her for her money!

TWO CALLERS FROM BRITISH RAILWAYS

Lord Eliot says No to a horse float

Express Staff Reporter

LORD ELIOT, 34-year-old heir to an earldom and owner of a racing stable, was taking after lunch coffee in his Wiltshire home. He was interrupted by his gardener.

"Two porters are outside," said the gardener.

Lord Eliot put down his coffee-cup and stepped into the yard of Grey Flags, Upavon.

The yard is flanked by stables for ten racehorses. Drawn up in the centre was a maroon-painted horse-float.

On its side was the inscription: "British Railways."

Said Lord Eliot: "The two men in porters uniforms said they wanted to show me the

ELIOT, Major Lord Nicholas Richard Michael Eliot; b. 26 Jan. 1914; s. s. of 8th Earl of St. Germans, q.v.: — *Educ.* : at great expense to his parents. *Recreations*: bustin' the slipper, shootin' a line, fishin' for compliments. *Address*: c/o Lloyds Bank.

—*from Who's Who, 1948.*

horse-float as an advertisement. Perhaps I would like to send my horses to the races by British Railways.

"I took one look. Then I said: 'To hell with this. I'm not a Socialist; I'm a Conservative. Take this float out of my yard. I'm for private enterprise.'"

Added Old Etonian Lord Eliot: "There they were: wasting petrol advertising a float, while private operators can't get enough petrol to do pukka transport jobs to racecourses.

"For the six months I have owned this place my horses have gone by private float. I can assure you they will go on doing so for the rest of my career."

If more turn up—

Lord Eliot, who served with the Duke of Cornwall's Light Infantry and the Royal Armoured Corps, went on:—

"If any more uniformed flunkeys from British Railways turn up in my yard with any sort of horse-float, they will leave very smartly.

"It still makes me mad to think of it."

The float that visited Lord Eliot (family motto : Press close upon those who take the lead)

LORD ELIOT
" *It still makes me mad. . . .* "

is one of a hundred owned by British Railways.

A spokesman for the railways executive said yesterday: "Horse-floats are going round the country, and in the course of things advertising visits are made to attract business."

Lord Eliot, elder son of the eighth Earl of St. Germans, is teamed up with trainer Charles Bell at Upavon. He spent part of last year in stables at Epsom "learning the game."

Two horses from his stable won over the sticks last week

1952 Peter o'Sullivan
Article
Daily Express

... the total to 102, but I do not think it would be unfair to say that had Charlie Smirke been available to ride Minstrel Queen (beaten by Fast Gal in the 4.30) Doug's score for the season would have read 101.

7lb. LESS

As Rene Emery is unable to " do " 10st. 7lb. just now, the services of " Tony " Bowles will reduce Pretty Fair's weight by 7lb. at Wincanton today. Whether this will be sufficient to give him a chance I doubt. But I hope.

Finally, an item from which you may derive more amusement than I. Following Pretty Fair's speeding offence while travelling to Wolverhampton, his owner was apprehended for a similar misdemeanour while driving to Yarmouth yesterday. . . . Would that my selections could exceed 30 miles an hour in the area built round the stands.

PRETTY INDIGNANT

AT least we did not lose any money on Pretty Fair yesterday.

"TONY " BOWLES, his intended rider, having been offered the job of travelling some horses to America for the London Bloodstock Agency over the week-end, not unnaturally accepted this alternative engagement.

But I gather Pretty Fair was pretty indignant to feel that a jockey was prepared to go to such lengths as to leave for America to avoid partnering him at Wincanton.

✱ ✱ ✱

Daily Express 1948
First year at Upavon

The labour government had nationalised all industry

Lord Eliot

Tony aged 15

Bath Winners
For Apprentice Riders

A. BOWLES SHINES ON CHWARAU TEG

By MEYRICK GOOD

THE continued drought has been giving trainers a lot of concern of late, but those running horses at Bath yesterday could not complain on the score of the going, as there was an excellent covering to the Lansdowne track.

Both going to the post and in the races the horses appeared to be striding out well.

Apprentice riders were in the limelight, three having winners.

The Kelston Handicap was won easily by Chwarau Teg, who has run well on the course before. C. Bell's apprentice Tony Bowles ride a very good race on the winner.

Bowles overcame a bad draw by getting his mount smartly away and being with the leaders into the straight. When Cream Cracker weakened Chwarau Teg raced smoothly into the lead.

3.0—KELSTON HANDICAP of £345; 2nd £100 3rd £50. One mile

CHWARAU TEG, ch h by Fairhaven—Triskeles, by Colorado Kid (Mr D T Farmiloe), 7-7-9* .... A Bowles 1
PERSIAN GLORY, b c by Turkhan—Luzerne (Mr A K D Butt), 4-8-11
.... F O'Neill 2
ELECTRICITY BILL, ~ c by William of Valence—Firey Light (Maj P Pearson-Gregory), 4-7-2 ...... F Sharpe 3
Providential (Mr N Webb), 7-8-2
.... Cliff Richards 4
Prince Richard (Lord Moynihan), 6-8-5
.... S Wragg 5
Cream Cracker (Mr J Ismay), 4-7-12
.... H Packham 6
Supersonic (Mr D Duncan-DuBno), 4-7-2* .... W Snaith 7
Sal o' Mine (Mr J Bowden), 4-6-10
.... T Grogan 8
Haberdasher (Mr G Smalley), 4-8-0 (car 8-1)............. P J Crawley 9
Knight of the Roses (Mr L P Freedman), 4-8-13 .... J Atkins 10
Kutgrass (Mr A Dingwall), 5-7-11*
.... P Mansbridge 0
Renardiere (Mr R W Sharples), 4-8-1*
.... J Walker 0
Blue Falls (Mr W Harvey), 4-8-4
.... T Weston 0
Countryman (Mr J Read), 4-7-5
.... H Oliver 14
Winner bred by Lt-Col D G F Darley; trained by C Bell. at Upavon, Wilts

(Off 3.5.)
S.P.: 6-4 Cream Cracker, 7-2 Prince Richard, 13-2 CHWARAU TEG, 7 Persian Glory, 8 Supersonic, 10 Haberdasher, 100-8 Kutgrass. Blue Falls, Providential, 100-6 Renardiere. 33 others. TOTE: 12/6; ol 5/.. 7/3, £4/18/0.

The Race: Kutgrass was slowly away. Sal o' Mine set the pace to Knight of the Roses, Haberdasher, Cream Cracker, Renardiere, and Persian Glory. At half-way Persian Glory went to the front, followed by Renardiere, Cream Cracker, Chwarau Teg. Providential, and Electricity Bill.

Shortly after rounding the final bend, Chwarau Teg raced into the lead from Persian Glory, while Prince Richard, Electricity Bill, and Providential moved up to challenge. Prince Richard was soon beaten, and Chwarau Teg easily held off the challenge of Persian Glory to win by four lengths; a short head Time, 1min 42

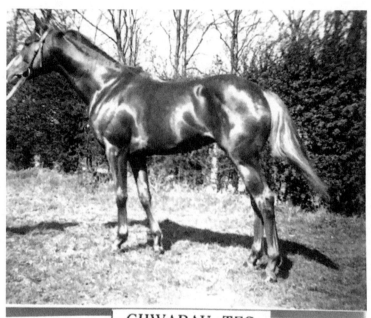

CHWARAU TEG
ATONES

APPRENTICE SHINES
AT BATH

" Tony " Bowles, C. Bell's apprentice,
rode a splendid race on Chwarau Teg
to win the Kelston Handicap at Bath

First ride ever at Lewes Finished 3rd

1946

Lewes

This was a bad day for me. I still have the scar from the fall in the first race, got left in the second and there was the biggest storm during the last race. The worst I've experienced.

1949

This was a bad day for me. Slipped up in the first race and got left in the second and there was a storm during the last race. The worst I've experienced.

Warwick Races

Weighing Room

**Grey Flags Racing Stables
Upavon Wiltshire 1948**

**Grey Flags
Upavon Wiltshire 1948**

**Charlie Bell Racehorse Trainer
1948**

**Some of the Lads in Yard
John Carter on Far Right
Tony next to him (1948)**

Tony with 3 year old filly "Lavevnoch" 1948

CONSCRIPTION

Call up had arrived. Which station was it? I forget, but I do remember there were 3 train loads going to Oswestry and most of the lads on board were Teddy Boys. The trains were going all day and I was on the one that left London mid-morning. I have never seen so many young lads and when we arrived the buses kept running all day. There must have been hundreds of potential soldiers. When we got to the camp we had to file through these huge sheds and there were loads of benches with soldiers stood behind waiting to serve you with your kit. The first one gave me a kit bag plus a sack, the next one wanted to know what size shirt I was. I had to have just three shirts plus one tie. The next lad wanted to know what head size I was bringing out two berets; next was trouser and chest size. We were handed two tunics and two pairs of trousers. Then came the socks, two pairs of horrid boots and the worst undergarments I had ever seen which ended up feeling like rasps on your skin! Lastly, I was given cleaning gear and cap badges; I could hardly walk carrying it all! I was allocated a billet allowing me somewhere to work on my gear and also sleep. The lance corporal was in the billet to let us know that he was in charge, sticking his nose right in our faces. He showed us how to buff our boots so that they would shine like a mirror. We were given all day to do this, but we still had to keep working at it for two weeks every evening.

The next morning at 6.30am I couldn't believe my ears at the noise outside; it was the sergeant running his batten along the billet walls. We had ten minutes to get outside for breakfast; no-one ever messed with these guys. When the parade and foot slogging started it was awful. It used to upset the Teddy Boys so much but no-one could do a thing about it. The next morning after we arrived, the queues were 50 yards long for the barbers and the regimental police were there. There was an RSM inside the barbers with his batten under his arm. You can imagine how the Teddy Boys felt with their lovely long hair and what they used to call their DA (Duck's Arse) at the back of their head. They were so accustomed to their hair that they would slip the barber 10 shillings for them not to take it all off. The barber would take the money from them and do what the lads wanted. Then the RSM would walk up to the barber in question stick his batten into the soldier's head and shout, "More off lad." They would be left with a small tuft on the top, leaving so many of these lads crying because their hair was their pride and joy! Some of the lads, who had never left home before, would end up crying in their beds at night. I could go on and on about the early training days, it was purgatory. Years later my grandson Ryan would enlighten me more on what went on being a regular soldier and he has so many stories to tell.

After so many weeks of training I would go through a series of interviews in front of a panel being asked what I would like to do in the army. "King's Troup with the horses for me please." The officer asked me why and I just said, "I don't know anything else sir," to which he replied, "You don't know much then do you son?" I got my wish and was transferred to St John's Wood in London, the home of the King's Troup. My first job was clipping horses, something which I was really chuffed about. No more training and I could travel home to West Ewell at the weekends – wishful thinking! I was only there for a couple of weeks, not even enough time to get my service dress uniform when Major Weldon called me into his office and explained what was going to happen to me. He told me that they were overloaded and couldn't keep me but he had found a good position for me as a groom to a Colonel Gillman at Larkhill Garrison in Wiltshire! Goodness me I thought, this just gets better and better as Larkhill is just a few miles from Upavon. On arriving at Larkhill I met the colonel, a very stern and abrupt man, but as it turned out a very fair man and more importantly, he took to me! All I had to do was look after two horses and the tack. A piece of cake I thought as having only been in the army a short time, here I was back in my favourite county. There were no parades even though the RSM tried and tried but I wasn't under his jurisdiction. It wasn't long before I was back in my old guvnor's house of an evening and riding out on my weekends off.

There were about ten grooms all allotted to different officers. I had never met such a different lot of fellows in my life involved with horses, coming from all walks of life all originating from St. Johns Wood. There were a few old scruffy soldiers there who were regulars and three of us doing our National Service. The sergeant and a bombardier were both very friendly and on first name terms with us all.

This was 1951 and I had started getting a few rides jumping for Mr Bell with the colonel's permission. My colonel was master of the RA foxhounds which met twice a week and I would ride second horse. I would follow the hunt at a distance only walking but keeping them all in sight and when he needed me, he would wave his arm and I would then take the other horse back to camp. Sometimes I looked after three horses. We only went out for exercise once a day for 2 hours, riding one and leading one or two. Often, I used to pop them over a few small fences. One of the ones I was leading was a slow old jumper, so I used to let him go half a length in front of me so that we all landed together, that way he didn't pull my arm out of its socket! All good fun. I was really enjoying looking after the army horses which were a lot different to racehorses and there were nearly always 12 of us on 2 hours exercise. If we went in the direction of Stonehenge then we would stop for a cuppa and sometimes we went around all the villages. My pal was a Scottish lad called Jock Rennie and he looked after a horse his major used for 'tent pegging'. Tent pegging was used in tournament competitions. There would be a wooden peg which is stuck into the ground and the rider, who has a 6ft lance at a gallop, has to pierce the tent peg. Jock and I used to train the major's horse and we would take it in turns to ride at a gallop trying to pick up the peg with the lance or to split it. You had to be so careful not to stick the lance in the ground. Once you had achieved this you had to swing the lance behind your shoulder and finish up with it in front of you. The horse had to be taught to keep a straight line and not flinch when you waved the lance around. Our job was to get the horse used to the lance and all of the army horses were good, not taking much training. For Jock and I this was a real fun time, making the best of our conscription!

One day when I saw Mr Bell, he told me that he had spoken to Frank Horris, a trainer of jumpers for a very big stable called Druid's Lodge. This stable was owned by a very rich man called J.A. Rank who owned 100 flat racehorses and quite a few good jumpers. This was a wonderful training establishment just two miles from Larkhill. Mr Bell had a word with Mr Horris and made arrangements for me to ride out if I wanted to. This was such a good opportunity so off I went to see him; he was such a nice man with a lovely wife. They were both quite elderly and they asked if I could manage riding out Wednesday mornings at 8am which was their morning for schooling. I now had the problem of asking the colonel but as it turned out it wasn't a problem as all he wanted was me to arrange cover for the time I was gone. I got myself an old bike and every Wednesday I would cycle past Stonehenge. My goodness, passing there in the dark was a bit spooky. I used to school the horses over the hurdles having breakfast with Mr and Mrs Horris afterwards. When I got back it was meal time and I had to pass the guardhouse where the RSM had his office to get to the cookhouse. I always knew that my face never fitted with him because he used to put me on orders for early morning parades which I just ignored. My colonel told me to take no notice as my job was to look after his horses. So rather than pass his office, as he was always looking out for me, I found a back way to the cookhouse. If he did catch me, he would go all over my dress and put me on a charge. He never did carry out his threat as I think he would have been worried about the backlash from the colonel. He harassed me from the day I arrived until the day I left so I just used to keep out of his way. The other lads would tell me if I was on orders for early morning parades and I would then talk to my colonel. He would say to me, "Well Bowles, what are you doing here then?" I would then say, "Looking after your horses sir," to which he would reply, "Quite right Bowles, it's just a misprint so take no notice!" I also had a friend in Brigadier General Cahoon because I looked after his little daughter's pony now and again. There is nothing like being in with the big wigs so they say, and they did think a lot of me.

Managing to get time off to ride out for Mr Horris and Mr Bell I was starting to enjoy my life in the army, doing my bit for King and Country! One Wednesday I was late getting there so the lad in the yard had the horse I was to exercise all ready for me. The lad told me that Mr Horris would meet me on The Gallops. The horse I was to ride that day was called 'Prince Regent'. Although he had finished racing, he was still going out for exercise. I can safely say that Prince Regent was the best horse that I ever rode out; he carried his head on the floor. For a horse that carried 12stone 7lb in the Grand National and finished 2nd, he was not as big as I thought he would be.

My Scottish pal Jock and I had lots of fun and laughs with the other lads and grooms. Jock and I used to get up to a lot of mischief, one of our favourites being catching the rats that managed to get into the horse's feed. There were four of these feeds in bins and we collected them mid-morning. One for midday, one for 4pm and one for late evening, the final one being for the following early morning feed. When they had one feed you would place the empty tin beneath the full ones, but once the final feed of the day had been used, we used to put the one for the morning underneath the empty ones. When we started work next morning the first thing we did was feed them that one. Sometimes the rats would be in that bin as you could hear them in there scratching around, how they got in there is a real mystery to me. So, before we fed our horses Jock and I would carry the tins with the rats into the billet. The lazy men were still in bed so we let the rats loose in the room and closed the door. You can imagine there was hell to pay! I was really upset when Jock was demobbed as it took away a lot of the fun.

One day I had permission to go racing and ride a horse for my old guvnor and this was over hurdles and I had a terrible fall. It was a mile and half race for 3-year-olds and the ground was very slippery. I landed so fast that I couldn't stop sliding, eventually turning over and a horse following fell on top of me. I lay there in a lot of pain waiting for the course ambulance and it was ages coming so I decided to get up and walk! The first aid room strapped my shoulder to travel home, but I had broken my collar bone. My colonel was not very pleased as he never expected me to come back injured. Consequently, I still had to look after my horses with one arm. I found this so very hard having to put the tack on etc. I even had to ride out with one arm. A month later the army medical officer took my strapping off and made me put my clothes on and get on with it. I had no warm therapy treatment so I was very sore and stiff.

In the summer, my colonel opened White City Horse of the Year Show with his RA foxhounds. I had to take my horses up to London with a couple more lads and their officers' horses. We were billeted with the Household Cavalry at Knightsbridge, a real eye opener! While I was up there, I met a lovely young girl who was there with her guvnor's showjumpers. Her name was Mary Reeves and she wrote to me all the time I was in the army; it was great getting a letter once a week. She did ask me to go and stay when I had leave, but when that came round, I was riding, so I never did.

One day, when riding schooling at Druid's Lodge, Mr Horris said he had 2 rides for Mr J.A. Rank for me at Wincanton so would I ask for time off. My colonel agreed but told me that if I didn't ride a winner then I would have no more time off to go racing. One of the horses didn't run because he had hurt himself out exercising. The other one did run, a 3-year-old called 'Box of Tricks'. It was a 2-mile hurdle race finishing unplaced after making the running for about a mile. I was riding to orders as Mr Horris had told me to let him run on in front if I could, but once the other horses came to him, he just didn't want to know. He was a horse that never liked racing, a pig of a horse in fact! While in the army I only ever rode for Mr Bell or J.A. Rank. Just my luck that Mr Rank died 2 weeks later and the whole establishment went up for sale. It was so huge that they had to split it up into 3 lots and that was besides what he owned in Ireland! His wife did end up keeping a few horses in training at Epsom with Mr Walter Nightingale and one of these horses was their Derby entry 'Gay Time' ridden by Lester Piggott. It finished second to a horse called 'Tular' ridden by Charlie Smirk. The irony is that I would have most likely have had a good job when I came out of the army had Mr Rank not passed away! However, I did manage to wear the colours of one of racing's biggest, richest and most successful owners!

My colonel asked me if I would look after a horse for 2 weeks, it belonged to a friend of his who was stationed there for a while. I couldn't refuse; I had been looking after him for just a week and was due to go on leave when he contracted colic. I spotted all the signs. He was restless, sweating up and trying to lay down. When this happens, all you can do is keep them on the move and not let them lay down. If they did, they would roll and end up twisting their gut, which in those days would have meant they would have to be shot. Maybe nowadays they would operate. I kept him walking nearly all day, as every time I took him inside, he wanted to lay down. I also gave him a couple of colic drinks which the vet made up for me. Again, this only eased it a little but towards tea time he seemed to be getting a little better so I left him for an hour, but always watching him on and off. He didn't want to eat but I did, so I went and got myself something then went back and walked him again until later into the evening. I took him in and let him loose in the box, he seemed quite comfortable so I left him and went to bed. I was due to go off early the next morning on a week's leave so I poked my head in to see how he was. He was stood in the corner of the box nice and quiet. I also checked on my other horses then made my way to Salisbury station. When I returned after my leave one of the lads told me I had missed all the fun while I was away!! I asked him where the horse with colic had gone. He said, "He has gone all right, he is dead!" I just couldn't believe it so he proceeded to tell me what had happened. Apparently, he wasn't properly over the colic and started getting pain again during the night ending upon the floor and injuring his inside. They kept walking him but the captain who owned him came to look at him and said he couldn't handle any more of this. The horse was obviously not insured otherwise he would have called for the vet. This would have been so much more humane as it would have been over in a matter of seconds, but he said he would go and get his gun and shoot him. "He only came back with a rifle," said the lad. The captain told the lad to hold him steady and he went around the front of him and shot him in the head and the bullet came out of his neck. The lad had a real job holding onto him, but he did it as best he could and the captain had another shot and this time he dropped down. The captain told the lad that he never wanted to do that again to which the lad replied, "Me neither." On reflection, I am just so very pleased that I went on leave as I couldn't have handled anything like that. When in the army you couldn't say anything about what went on to your superiors of course.

Another time I travelled two horses overnight to Portland Down for a hunt taking place the following day and I did this on my own leaving mid-afternoon crossing Salisbury Plain. I arrived there about half an hour before the cookhouse closed, so I quickly made sure the horses were fine in order to get there before it shut. I ran across the parade ground which, on reflection, was not a good idea as of course I was spotted by the RSM. He roared at me, "You there, stand to attention. Do you know why I stopped you soldier?" "Yes sir, for running across the parade ground," I replied. "Quite right soldier. Now put your arms above your head and run around the square until I tell you to stop." He returned ten minutes later and told me to go about my business. Sod's law. By the time I got to the cookhouse it was closed. I knocked on the door and explained my situation and was informed that all they had left was two kippers, bread and jam. I would have been pleased with anything as I was starving so I had it all. It was so good that I even ate the bones!

The meeting started at 10am the following day. I followed

the hunt on one of the horses for my colonel to change over when he needed to. When returning, his first horse was worn out so we staggered home.

On another occasion the same thing happened again. This time after my colonel had changed horses, we were right across the other side of Salisbury Plain meaning I had about an hour's ride to get back to Larkhill. Halfway home a really bad mist came down and I couldn't see 5 yards in front of me, consequently I couldn't pick out any landmarks, couldn't see any holes or trenches so you can imagine I was in a right state. I eventually arrived back about 10pm and the hunt had been finished for ages. I got my horse back in his stable the other one had been looked after by one of the other soldiers. My colonel had arrived back about 6pm as he went back another way and didn't hit the mist. When he saw me the next morning and asked what had happened, I told him and he laughed his head off!

When on leave from the army I used to go home and ride out for different trainers in Epsom. Just before I was due to get demobbed, I had a letter from Mary saying that she didn't think our relationship was going anywhere, something which I agreed with. Hence, no more lovely letters from her which I had enjoyed so much but I wasn't too upset really.

My colonel asked me what I wanted for a leaving present, something special. I had no hesitation in saying that I would really like a nice stick or whip for riding out exercise. He bought me the most beautiful leather-bound whalebone whip with a gold band around it with my initials on it. Leaving him was a little upsetting, but getting out of the army was just wonderful. Now I had to get my thinking cap on to decide what I was going to do.

In February 1953, to achieve my discharge papers, I needed to go back to The King's Troop and work three more days. In the end they didn't need me so gave me my papers straight away along with a travel warrant and the address of the Territorial Army Unit in Sutton. I was to report there for my 3 years in the TA for 2 weeks' training every year plus 3 weekends a year. What a load of rubbish that was!

I was now home in West Ewell with nothing to do but relax and decide where I was going with my life. I knew I was getting nowhere with Mr Bell, however, on the other hand he had stood by me and given me rides. He only had a handful of jumpers so the question I asked myself was should I go back or not? I decided that, because I enjoyed the village life so much and I had great digs, I would go back. Everyone was so pleased to see me and Mr Bell was so happy to have me back with him. I used to do nearly everything from running the yard to helping Mr Bell with the entries, these entries being sent to Wetherby's in London. By the time the jumping season finished all I had was about 8 rides with the best finish being third, but this didn't stop me enjoying the country life. Then there was a very big upset for Mr Bell as Lord Eliot was selling the house and yard and going back to living at his London club and his estate in Cornwall. Mr Bell now had the problem of where to go with his horses. As it happened, he was friendly with a big businessman in the village called Mr Andrews. He owned the local travelling horseboxes and also owned the rabbit rights with contracts to all the local butchers and different restaurants. He also used to have a horse in training with Mr Bell. He told him not to worry and that he would build a yard for him and his 14 horses on a piece of his land. By the time 'Grey Flags' was sold we were in the new yard, so lucky old Mr Bell.

I reported to Sutton for 2 weeks training in the TA; as far as I was concerned this was a waste of time. I was driven to a camp in Wales near the Brecon Beacons which seemed to take hours in the truck. The first week consisted of marching, gun training and training on mortars with the last week going on manoeuvres on the Beacons. My job was on mortars being the one who puts the bomb down the barrel.

We got to the gun positions just before midnight, having to set these up ready for firing in the morning. Then we went into a derelict building to sleep and I was so very tired I couldn't wait to get to sleep, but no such luck. All the other crews were playing cards and this encouraged my crew to start playing cards together as well. They wouldn't let me go to bed, so I had to play brag with them. I was getting all the good hands and winning all the money in the kitty. Try as I might I couldn't get them to win it back so went to bed with all their money, about £50 of it! Poor blokes, but their fault for making me play, I was not a popular chap after that but at least they never asked me to play again.

During the next day two of the bombs never exploded, so I had to carry these bombs 50 yards to the nearest trees, nearly sh.....g myself. One thing I did see and really appreciated on the Beacons was a herd of wild ponies in the distance, and to my amazement I saw two stallions round them up and take them elsewhere. I have never seen this before or since, such a wonderful sight.

Now being back in Upavon where the summers were always good during the '50s it was very hot as were the local girls! Having Tony Keen as a mate the summer seemed to go really quickly. I was enjoying my life so much stuck in a tiny village in the middle of Wiltshire. At this time the local owners of the land and the farmers in Upavon and the local council decided to put on a Fun Day in Upavon and to run a Carthorse Derby. So, Tony Keen and I asked a local farmer if we could borrow two of his Clydesdales. He told us we were welcome to them as long as we used no whips. The bookmakers were taking bets and there were about 8 runners. The race was won by a light weight carriage horse, but it was later disqualified as the bookmakers refused to pay out because it wasn't a carthorse! The race was re-run and I went to the nearest hedge, picking myself a little branch with leaves on, as you couldn't get these Clydesdales out of a trot unless you coaxed them. I won the race and beat Tony Keen by a short head.

By the time the jumping season arrived in 1953/54 the winter was so very cold and more especially when riding out as there was not much shelter on the Downs.

I received a letter from Mr George Warren who was an Epsom trainer asking me to go and be stable jockey for him. He knew me as I had ridden out for him when on leave from the army. The next day I was going racing to ride a horse for Mr Bell so I told him about my letter. He was reading The Sporting Life and showed me what was written about Mr Warren. It was front page news that he had been warned off for doping; yet another missed opportunity for me!

It was the beginning of November and I had only had 3 rides when Mr Bell told me I had a ride the following week for Peter O'Sullivan. It was a lovely little fella called 'Pretty Fair' who jumped well and most certainly had a winning chance. Mr Bell told me that they didn't fancy him, meaning that he wouldn't be trying. Well, that same evening Walter (Wally), Mum's new husband rang me to ask if I would fancy going to America travelling 10 yearlings with him and 3 other lads for the London Bloodstock. I didn't need to think about this as I just knew it would be something really special. All I had to do was get a passport, which did prove to be a rush and a lot of hassle, but it was well worth it. Once this was done, I went to see Mr Bell in the evening but he had gone to bed. He put his head out of the bedroom window to ask what I wanted. I told him and he agreed, but he was worried about the ride I had the following week for Peter O'Sullivan as he knew he would be upset. Of course, I didn't feel good about doing this to either of them but I really couldn't miss this great opportunity. I just felt this was my destiny. The day 'Pretty Fair' was due to run I looked at the Daily Express and noticed it was a non-runner. Peter O'Sullivan was very upset with me, and being a correspondent for the Daily Express he wrote in his article that day, "Tony Bowles would rather be a few thousand miles away than ride my horse."

TRAVELLING HORSES ABROAD

Living back home again and working for the London Bloodstock I found myself on a plane travelling horses to America. Bearing in mind that I had never even flown before and this was a big clipper with four props! We loaded up 10 yearlings and when we taxied to the end of the runway at Heathrow and the pilot revved up the engines, I nearly wet myself! The yearlings also wondered what was happening as everything on the aircraft was shaking and falling about. It's really difficult to describe what it was like. The year was 1953 and we were one of the pioneers of racehorse transport to America. Our first stop was Shannon to refuel and load the mail, second stop was Reykjavik for more fuel and then last stop Ganda to refuel again! The journey took 12 hours in all to get from London to New York. Once in America we went through 3 separate interrogation rooms before we got the thumbs up and this all took another 2 hours! When we stopped at Shannon, we picked up a chap who had taken a brood mare over for Florence Nightingale Graham and was travelling back to

New York. Florence's business name was 'Elizabeth Arden' the rich cosmetic queen who also owned many racehorses. On the way over we started chatting along with Wally about jump jockeys etc. He said that this lady was looking for a jump jockey as all of the American jockeys were drinkers and smokers. So, Wally took the opportunity and told him that I never drank or smoked and had ridden winners on the flat and over the jumps. He told Wally that, on arrival in New York her agent would be waiting for him to give him a ride back and he would introduce us, which he duly did. On introducing me he told the agent that I might be just the lad that they were looking for. The agent said that he would discuss this information with Miss Graham and would meet us at the airport before we returned to England and let us know what she said. When he met us, he said that she would employ me and the wages would be good! Unfortunately, I didn't have the confidence or the guts to do this and I knew I wouldn't be able to handle it, so I refused. Once again, I missed out, but this was my fault being my first trip abroad and I was a very immature 22-year-old.

When we got to New York we had the long trip to the city as the airport was Idlewild (which was renamed John F Kennedy airport in 1963). We checked into our hotel called

'Dixieland' on 42nd street, had a quick shower and went up Broadway for a meal and a look around. There were four of us, Wally, Ted Freed, myself and another lad whose name escapes me. We ate wonderful food which was also very cheap, a very different world to what I was used to. We finished up at Jack Dempsey's Bar and Restaurant, this was some place. Unfortunately, Jack wasn't there, but we sat at the bar which was shaped like a horseshoe and I thought to myself, this is the life! We all went shopping the next day and ended up buying things which we couldn't buy back home. I remember buying myself a lovely suede jacket for just a few dollars. We went to a show at Radio City's big music hall and also to Grand Central Station, then walking up 5th Avenue where all the top designers have their shops (out of our league but good to see).

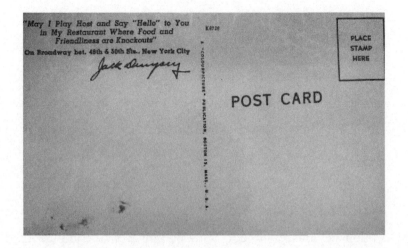

We returned to the airport the next day and had a good trip home arriving back at 3am and having to wake Customs up as we flew back on a freight flight! Working for the Bloodstock full time also involved going to the Newmarket sales and returning to Epsom the horses that were bought for buyers to be shipped abroad. The next trip for me was Caracas, Venezuela, taking 10 brood mares that I didn't know and lads that I didn't know also. We did have a young veterinary surgeon with us which was compulsory transporting brood mares. This takes some believing but we had to unload the brood mares on the tarmac at Idlewild in New York and put them on another plane bound for Caracas before we continued. I think the whole journey took about 16 hours but I did enjoy it. We flew quite low over Rio de Janeiro and the approach to Caracas airport is the most beautiful sight as you come in across a lovely bay just off the Caribbean. When the cargo doors were opened the humidity hit us and we found it hard to breathe. There were people there to take over from us so we made our way to the city as the transport was all laid on. They did tell me the only worry for the brood mares were snakes. If the mares, when turned out in the fields, happened to tread on them they would give them a deadly bite. We stayed in a classy hotel but didn't have much time to sightsee, however what I did see were glorious sights I had never seen before; such a rich country but with so many poor people. These people were being ruled by a Dictator or El President. Walking up the main street there were so many police and the army all with guns, which was very intimidating. Little boys used to pop out from the side streets propositioning us to go and see their lovely sisters, which of course we didn't! The young vet who was with us decided that he would take photos of everything. We were passing this big building called the El Presidente and he was snapping away when suddenly the palace was surrounded by armed guards. A truck pulled up and grabbed him and we never saw him until we were on the flight going home. They escorted the young vet up the steps onto the plane after they had questioned him and confiscated his film. I thought to myself, "What a berk!" We had a good laugh about it on the flight home.

As part of my job working for the London Bloodstock, I also took one or two racehorses at a time to the London Docks as these horses were going to Australia. I can remember, on more than one occasion, that the dockers had been on a 'work to rule' which meant that they weren't hurrying, they were playing cards etc. The horses didn't end up getting on the ship that day so we had to take them back to the yard and go up the following day. They ended up being loaded in a loose box by crane which lifted the box up onto the deck where it was fastened to the deck and all this took about half an hour. They all travelled like this on the deck for the whole journey. On other occasions, I loaded them below deck walking all through the steel corridors. This was a very hard job to do as well as all the iron corridors were not even 5 feet wide. The best way to travel would be on deck but I did hear when the weather was really rough the horses could be swept overboard. The one thing I enjoyed was the tea and food at the docks. The dockers did tell that to get a job there it was more or less a family concern, so I had no chance doing that then! The worst thing was all the hanging about.

Another one of my trips was to travel up to Hollyhead to meet the boat train from Ireland that was travelling with 2 brood mares. From Hollyhead I took them to the Queen's Stud at Sandringham. I booked into a hotel for 2 nights due to the rough Irish Sea and used to go to the railway docks and sit in a café all day waiting. It arrived on the 3rd day. The carriage was put into a siding waiting for the train to pick it up so I had to run to the hotel and collect my bag and pay my bill. When the train picked the carriage up from the station, I settled down with them on the train and the journey took 12 hours! I was suffering from the flu while I was there, so everything was done with great difficulty. A total of 3 times we got shunted into sidings for a couple of hours to go onto another line. This did mean that I could go and get a sandwich and a hot drink though and get back in time before it took off without me. Once I arrived at Sandringham an old stud groom of about 70 met me and took me to his cottage to stay the night. His housekeeper was his spinster daughter and the cottage was just like something out of Dickens! No electric just candles, but I did have good food! Before I left in the morning I saw this magnificent horse galloping around a small paddock, a paddock just for him. This horse was called 'Auriol' which was the Queen's Stallion who finished 2nd in the Derby to Pinza and won the King George and Queen Elizabeth stakes at Ascot.

By the time I got home my flu had gone. This was the least pleasant job I did for the Bloodstock and I know I had it because I was the last man joining the firm and no one else wanted it – surprise, surprise! I would never advise anyone to spend a week in Hollyhead.

Another small job I had was helping Mr Chamberlain, the vet, some Sunday mornings in the winter just after Christmas. He used to castrate the yearlings for some of the Epsom trainers. It was just him and me doing this job, which meant the lads in the different stables could go home and leave us to it. He would give me about £20 per session, which was very good money for about one and a half hours work and we would do about 6 yearlings in an hour. We would then go to the local pub and he bought me a beer saying, "We deserve that!" He was a man in his 60's about 6 feet 2 inches tall and grossly overweight, therefore he couldn't get down to do the job, all he did was feel! The horses were never stitched up, just washed out by the lads in the afternoon and this was a nice little earner for me.

Early in 1954, while still working for the London Bloodstock, one lunchtime Wally and I went to the Amato pub which is at the bottom of Chalk Lane in Epsom. While we were there having a drink a little old man came in who we both recognised as Charlie Grey, an old jockey. We bought him a drink and he was delighted. He was very smart in a suit, collar and tie and shoes that shone, but you could see that everything he had on was old but well looked after. He now lived in The Alms Houses at Dorking Road Hospital in Epsom. We sat at his table and had the most interesting conversation; he must have been about 84 at the time. He had ridden in many different countries riding Derby winners as well as having rides at every racecourse in the UK. The best story for me was him having ridden in races with the great Fred Archer – my idol. I am so very lucky to possess a form book that confirms every word Charlie said. I thought this was so marvellous to have had a chat with a jockey who had ridden in those days, being the late 1800's.

Later that year when we had a slack period Wally suggested I ride out for Mr George Warren to keep my hand in, although he had been warned off, he still had a couple of horses in the yard. Off I went and rode one of his jumpers schooling and afterwards Mr Warren would take me home for breakfast and I met his lovely wife. Wally, who was in charge of the Bloodstock yard, said they were still not busy, so maybe it would be better if I rode out all week for Mr Warren. Whilst riding out for him I thought it was no good keep taking my lovely leather whalebone whip home and bringing it back again, so I left it in the saddle room. One of the worst decisions I have ever made, but I never thought for one minute it would come to harm. Some of Mr Warren's old lads used to call in to say hello and I never knew this and the thing was they were right villains, so my whip vanished. I was so upset as was Mr Warren when I told him, but it was my own fault for leaving it there and being so trusting. When I told Wally he said he thought he knew who it would have been but without proof what can you do? Now, in hindsight, I should never have used it and then it would have pride of place on my wall right now.

Shortly before Christmas I was riding out this jumper and it was entered in a race on Boxing Day and Mr Warren asked me to ride it. Although he now wasn't officially allowed to train it, another Epsom trainer called Mr John Benstead, being a mate of Mr Warren and also of the owner, offered to run it in his name. So off I go and get my orders from Mr Benstead and all he wanted me to do was get around safely and not to get hurt as if I did there would have been repercussions as what they were doing was illegal. Brother Pat drove me to Kempton and it ran well in a big field of runners (unbeknown to me at the time this was to be my last ride.)

I continued my work with Wally in the yard and in the meantime Mr Warren had packed up and moved to Canada. A local trainer called Jackie Sirett had given up riding as a jockey and started training in the yard where Mr Warren was. It just so happened that a very astute racing lad became head lad and his name was George Dunkley, a man I could not take to (not many could mind you!). George asked Wally to ask me if I would go and be travelling lad for them but I told Wally to say no way would I work with him.

My next trip for the Bloodstock (which turned out to be my last) was New York again. I was travelling a great big chaser which had been bought by an American to ride hunting on and he was the biggest I had ever seen, about 18 hands. The little filly was in foal and belonged to the Queen so just two animals, but all on my own. The sad part of it was that they would be waiting in a horsebox for me to collect at the airport. This was not good; it was always better to have them in your yard until they travelled abroad, this way they would be hungry and thirsty, so when loaded on board, that was all they would be thinking about, not worried about what is going on all around them. Wally came with me to help load them up. I led the big chaser up the ramp while it was very dark. I just managed to get him to duck his head down to get in the plane and he slipped up. He turned a somersault and the whole plane shook. Oh no I thought, that's a good start! I led him up the plane to the stalls; he stood in the stall which only came up to his chest at the top of his leg. I am on my own with this fella! The filly was a little darling, no trouble whatsoever as she stood in the stall next to him like a little pony! Wally said goodbye and good luck and gave me the medical box with the hypodermic needle in plus 6 phials of morphine. When the pilot came on board, he was carrying a big gun over his shoulder and he told me that if the big fella caused problems, he had no option but to shoot him! The big chaser kept threatening to do something terrible, getting all worked up, sweating like mad, so I kept pumping the morphine into him breaking a couple of needles. At last, he settled down and after about 3 hours of this I was really knackered, as you can imagine, so I sat in the seat and collapsed! Now here is a story that really beggars belief. The co-pilot was at the back of the plane asleep when the pilot came up to me and said, "Are you hungry fella?" Well of course I was starving. So, he told me to go into the cockpit and, "Fly the plane!" He told me he would show me what to do and that way he could go and make my sandwich! He sat me down in the pilot's seat and said, "Now, here's the stick — see the dials there, well just hold the stick steady keeping it on this line and it won't be a problem and I'll be back shortly!" This plane was a huge 4 prop clipper freighter and I did think this has got to be a joke! I am looking after 2 racehorses, one of whom could go bonkers at any time, it is pitch black outside and I am here in the cockpit! Looking out of the window it was just black and very frightening. Back came the pilot with this 3-tier sandwich and said, "OK fella, well done, now enjoy your sandwich," which I really did as it was like nectar to me. We got to New York safe and sound after about 12 hours, the big chaser had only threatened thank goodness. I was so pleased to get off and say my goodbyes to the pilot and the horses! It wasn't my job to get the horses off, transport had been arranged to do this. I booked my evening flight for the next day and got a taxi to New York and The Dixieland Hotel. It was just great to get into the shower and then off out up to Broadway to get a good meal. After my meal I wanted to try Jack Dempsey's bar again, but no luck as he wasn't there this time neither. I made my way back to my hotel and had a good evening there, getting myself a night cap and listening to this great blind resident pianist who had this lovely Alsatian dog lying beside him. Then off to my bed thinking about flying this huge transatlantic aircraft. It soon dawned on me that it was obviously on automatic pilot, or was it? The penny dropped, knowing the pilot's sense of humour, it would probably end up as one big joke in their club, a real talking point! The following day I had a nice walk-up Broadway after a hearty breakfast, but not much fun on my own so I just went to the airport.

Now I had been back working in the yard for a couple of weeks when the Bloodstock said they couldn't keep me on because they wouldn't be busy enough until the sale time at the end of the year. Now, as luck would have it, one of the Bloodstock directors was a big Epsom racehorse trainer.

He asked me if I would like to go and work for him during the summer and that way, I could go back to them for the sales. I thought that was a great idea as I did enjoy travelling the horses abroad. Hence, I started working for Mr Vic Smyth, but I got fed up as, although he was a big and successful trainer, he ran a ragtime firm. George Dunkley then approached me yet again to ask if I would work for Jackie Sirett as he really wanted me and couldn't get me quick enough. In fact, this was the 3rd time of asking and he did say he wouldn't ask me again. For reference, the Bloodstock Yard was called Caithness and Jackie Sirett's yard was in Portland House, just next door. Both yards were in Ashley Road, Epsom, next to Roseberry Park. So starts another era of my horseracing career.

TRAVELLING HEAD LAD

My travelling abroad days were no more and this was June 1955. Jackie only had about 5 horses. There was one paid lad, plus a boy, George, and now me. An apprentice called Jock Johnson, who was from Tommy Carey's yard, came along about a month after me (he had his indentures transferred). He was a very likable lad and we got on well and in fact remained friends until he died. Both Elaine and I are still very friendly with his wife, Gillian. He was a very good boxer and got through to the Championship Final for the Stable Lads. This was held at The Albert Hall and I went up and watched. I think the weight was about 7 stone 7lb and a coach was hired to take everyone. Also, Rex Wilkinson, another mate of mine, had reached the final of his weight. Again, both Elaine and I remained good friends with Rex as well; unfortunately both of these good boxers have sadly passed away. It was such a good night with marvellous boxing. Jock lost his fight against A.C. Rawlinson (who had beaten Terry Spinks previous). Terry left racing after this and turned professional and was to become British Featherweight Champion after he had won Olympic Gold!! Rawlinson's fight with Jock was a disputed decision so that just shows how good Jock was and both Jock and Rex were champion army boxers. I did meet

Terry Spinks at Kempton Park after he was champion; he came running across the paddock to make a fuss of me, but then asked me what I fancied!!

As far as my new job was concerned, it took me a little while to get into the swing of things as all this work was new to me. My job consisted of looking after the silks of different owners, plus paddock clothing for the horses and racing tack. Fortunately, with only a few horses, I soon learnt what was what and I was, surprisingly, getting on well with George! As the season progressed, we acquired a few more horses and another paid lad by the name of Tommy Millard; he had just come out of the army and was a year younger than me. Again, Elaine and I are very friendly with Tom and his wife, Shirley. I used to clip the horses, about 15 to 20 of them each winter and some of them had to be clipped twice. But now the machine was much improved and was electric, all I needed was a lad to hold the horses for me. We finished the season with 4 or 5 winners, pretty good for just a few horses. Jackie, being new to training, was good to work for and nice and easy going. At the end of the season, we moved stables and we went up to Treadwell Road to a place called Treadwell House Stables. This belonged to Mr Stanley Wootton and Jackie had served his apprenticeship with him. He was in

Australia at the time, as he had a big stud farm and also horses in training out there. He was one of our owners as well; also he owned most of the land around Epsom Downs and Headley including the gallops. At the end of the first year with Jackie I took 2 horses to the Bloodstock sales at Newmarket. While there, I went to see Mr Charlie Bell who was now a private trainer to the famous Miss Parsons. Her father designed engines for the Queen Mary. On one occasion, when it couldn't leave New York due to engine trouble, Miss Parsons flew out and helped fix the engines. All of the yearlings were exercising in the paddock and Mr Bell asked me if I would get on one and ride it around with the string and tell him what I thought of it. He also put me on 2 more to see what I thought; they were all lovely animals and he was so very fortunate to get this job. On the other hand, she was a very eccentric lady who had previously had a few trainers in Newmarket. She ended up sacking Bell before the flat season started. About a year later a lad who had worked for her, who she still owed wages to, murdered her, would you believe? The second year with Jackie I met Mr Wootton; he had just come back from Australia. He came in the yard one evening, shook my hand and told me he was pleased to meet me. He said that I should be sure to take care of Jackie as he knew nothing of looking after horses! As well as having horses in training with Jackie he also trained horses himself. I did many favours for him and he always praised me as being 'The Best'.

Christmas that year was good and I had generous presents (money). We also acquired more horses, buying a few yearlings at the sales and Lord Roseberry sent us four 3-year-olds and I was fortunate in getting to know him really well. I also had my own saddle room with all the travelling gear in it. 1956 came and we had a good season with 15 winners, now this may not sound like many, but they were all fancied so again that meant good presents! At the end of the year Tommy Millard left.

That same year brother Pat and I went in partnership with a new car and he taught me the basics of driving. At that time there was trouble in the Suez Canal so petrol was rationed and learner drivers were allowed to drive without someone beside them. So, I was driving for 6 months on my own and then passed my test 1st time, even though my examiner was a right tartare who was well known for not passing anyone 1st time! Anyway, she was 10 minutes late coming out to get me and when I saw who I had got my heart dropped! During the test she told me that I hadn't been looking in my mirror. I said to her, "Excuse me, but I beg to differ as I have been checking my mirror constantly." She told me not to argue with her. Apparently, I should have been moving my head not just my eyes, but I never knew that. Anyway, she did pass me and it was a feather in my cap!

Jockeys V Trainers

Back Row Left to Right
Ernie Sparrowhawk
Alan Oughton
Brian Swift
Gay Kindersley
Edward Underdown
Geoff Laidlaw
Vic Smythe
Bill Rees
Bob Parker
Mick Dillon
???
Dave Nicholson
Tony Bowles
Vic Smythe Junior
Harold Wallington Junior
Mr Sherwood

Front Row Left to Right
Geoff Lewis
Mark Griffith
Tommy Millard
Kevin Spence
Boggy Whelan
Bill Saye
Bunny Iodendon
???
Johny Gilbert

Cricket Match

During the summer I played cricket for the racing lads and we had a big match in the college grounds at Epsom. The lads versus celebrities, film stars and jockeys and all very official. I am sure the celebrities won; I still have a photo of the teams.

The first few years with Jackie were good, having lots of winners at Epsom. Uncle Pat would often go up on the hill and put my money on as well as some for himself. Mum had moved house to Banstead and Ann met and married Brian Knott.

In 1956 Mr Bell died and by this time he was living in Newmarket with his wife Dorothy. I drove myself and Wally there to the funeral and the crematorium was packed out. On the way home the car broke down, so we left it in a garage for repair and came back by train. When it was ready both Pat and I went and collected it and I paid for it as per usual!! Dorothy remained a good friend, a very lovely Lady.

During this time my brother met June Compton and married her in 1958. I was to be best man but we had runners on the day and there was no-one else to do my job! Consequently, David Anstee (Elaine's brother) stood in for me. I did manage to get to the reception in the evening which was held at June's mum and dad's in Randalls Road in Leatherhead. Who did I see there but Elaine who was chief bridesmaid. I had seen her once before when I picked June and Pat up when they were courting and actually had a feeling about her, but she was so young!! Therefore, I kept these feelings to myself, but when Elaine and I started courting she said she felt the same way even being so young. So, it was really meant to be, and all thanks to June and Pat.

Jackie moved yard again in 1959, buying his own property. It was a yard with a house in Langley Vale which he called 'Burnside' and it was a very cold yard in the winter. We did have a certain amount of luck to start with in this yard and also had quite a few good apprentices. I realised Jackie was changing his attitude towards training; he was not taking much notice of his head lad, George, who was marvellous at his job. He certainly didn't take any notice of me neither! I just carried on and enjoyed life. There was only one snag, and that was getting to and from work living in Banstead, it was so out of the way in those days. If it wasn't my turn to have the car and Wally wasn't there to give me a lift, I had to get the bus and the service was dreadful. As luck would have it, Mum decided to move back to Epsom to a flat near the town (she would always move if she needed cash!) Then one day Jackie said, if I would pick the lads up, I could use one of his cars, better than walking I thought to myself. Little did I know then that I was making a rod for my own back!

Now we get to 1960 and June and Pat were living in a maisonette in Epsom, so I decided that for a treat for Christmas I would take them to see a film in London. When I went to ask them, June was there alone and was delighted when I told her. But then she asked me who I would be taking, so I told her Shirley Groats who was very attractive and lived next door to us. June said if I took her, she didn't want to go, so I asked her who she thought I should take then! I was gobsmacked when she told me to ask Elaine! How do I manage to ask Elaine's parents with her being so young, just 16 and with me being 29? June told me I would have no problem, she knew they would say yes! So off I went to ask them and they did say yes and also asked me to sit down and have a whisky! Elaine wasn't there at the time but she came in later and was thrilled. I thought, is this a celebration or what? Well folks, that went rather well I thought. We went to London to see South Pacific and we all loved it. During 1960 Elaine and I saw a little more of each other as the year progressed. We were really enjoying getting to know each other better and having some fun. I don't know about the racing part of my life (although now I was seeing Elaine I wasn't too bothered) it seemed to be really up and down with not many winners and no winners meant no extra money of course and this was all down to bad horses. At this time my wages were £8 10 shillings a week and my travelling expenses were £1 10 shillings each time and for each winner we had I got £10. As the year progressed, we were having a few winners either ridden by Bryan Leyman or Michael Haines. This was all good for the lads.

Also this year, an old friend, Dickie Broadway, got married. Dickie was a good hurdle race jockey and came in the yard one morning and asked me to be his best man. He was living in Marlborough at the time and getting married there. He said to bring my mum and also Elaine. Of course, Wiltshire was familiar ground to me and we all enjoyed the wedding. Unfortunately, the next year poor Dickie, while riding at Cheltenham, caught his leg on the rails going around a bend. He smashed it up terribly and had operation after operation, but was never able to ride again.

In the winter of 1960 Mum had a phone call from Noreen her sister, who lived at 71, College Road, Epsom and looked after Grandad. She told Mum that Grandad had collapsed behind his bedroom door and she couldn't open it. I rushed over there and pushed the door open and

Noreen and I lifted him onto the bed but by this time he was dead. After the funeral we moved to 71 to live with Noreen. Also, I think it was this year, George was reading The Sporting Life one morning at work and saw that Tony Keen had been killed in a car accident. This was such a shock to me as I used to travel down to Upavon when I was on holiday to see him and spend time with him. Each time I saw him he had got engaged to a new girl; he was always in love!! He would always bring the girl of the moment with him to meet me. He was such a good pal and I missed him so much.

At the end of this year the London Bloodstock packed up, I suppose it just couldn't survive. It was such a high-class firm; everything was done for the best with nothing spared. I just think they never made it pay as they never cut corners. Consequently, Wally had to find another job and this was really hard for him as he had always had it so good with them.

During 1961 Elaine was at college training to be a hotel receptionist. But by the time she had finished and got her results she decided hotel work was not for her with the shift work. My hours were bad enough but with Elaine working shifts we would hardly see each other. So, she became a receptionist for Birds Eye frozen foods in

London and enjoyed it. When we were both on holiday, we used to visit Eckington near Sheffield to see Elaine's relatives. I fitted in very well with everyone and we both had a really good time.

I was working hard as travelling head lad, not having many winners though and therefore, not earning much money either. I did go away quite a lot with overnight runners; my favourite course was always Goodwood (although that was not an overnighter). I remember once when a lot of Elaine's relatives from Leatherhead went there on a coach trip and they went up on the hill, always a good place for seeing the horses walking around the paddock. The following weekend when I saw them, they were all very excited as they had seen me in the paddock standing next to the Queen! I felt quite famous from what they were saying to me!

I used to go swimming in the open-air pool at the end of Epsom or meet up with some of the lads down town during the afternoon before stables. Once a week I used to go and play crib with John Carter. Another evening I would go to Arthur and Josie Ring's in Epsom with a few other jockeys to play cards. Josie would go to bingo but not before she left us all some sandwiches and beer!

Getting near the end of the year I would go to the Yearling Sales in Newmarket and bring back the horses that Jackie Sirett had bought. Now that he was buying without advice, they never turned out much good really. We had to rely on Lord Roseberry and other big owners who bred their own to send us something good.

On August 29th 1961, Elaine's mum and dad celebrated their silver wedding at The Prince of Wales Pub in Leatherhead. My mum was also invited; she played the piano all evening which she loved. She could play any song. Someone only had to hum the tune and she would pick it up, so a good evening was had by all dancing and singing. As per usual, I had been racing so arrived late. Just after the party I asked her mum and dad if we could get engaged on Christmas Day as Elaine would be 18 then and they said yes! We went to Eckington in November staying with Elaine's relatives and bought the engagement ring. Elaine found the ring she wanted for exactly the price I told her I could afford which was £50. We did actually get engaged on Christmas Eve as I put the song 'True Love' on my record player and Elaine said, "Let's get engaged to this as it can always be our song." I actually went to midnight mass that year with Elaine, had never been before or since! Of course, Christmas was very special to us that year and we spent it at Elaine's auntie and uncle's house (Ruth and Bill Compton) with the extended family. On Boxing Day, we then all went to Elaine's mum and dad's and her mum had made us a lovely engagement cake. This was the start of a very bad winter with such a great deal of snow. We were all due to go to the British Legion to celebrate New Year but I couldn't get to Leatherhead due to the thick snow.

We always exercised the horses, even in the snow, but on these occasions we went through the back way from the yard which took us straight onto the Downs, so no road work. I had real difficulty getting to work and back and it was a really cold time all through this winter. I was bringing home about £11 per week for a 7-day week with just every other Sunday afternoon off compared to Elaine who was working a 5-day week in London and bringing home £39 per month, mind you, out of that she had to pay her travelling expenses. By the middle of January, we realised that Elaine may be pregnant so we both had the job of telling her mum and dad about the baby. In those days it was such a real stigma to be pregnant before you were married, mainly to do with what the neighbours would say! I thought her dad would be the one who would be most upset but he was really good and even took me down the cellar and poured me a whisky because he could see I was feeling really ill. Elaine's mum was a different kettle of fish; she hit the roof and also went to pieces. I could understand that really as Elaine, being their only daughter, they had always wanted her to have a big white wedding! But the main thing is that we were going to get married in any case at some stage, we did love each other and we were very happy about it all. Now it was a rush job to get it all arranged. I got a special license which meant we could get married in 3 weeks. Elaine was told not to tell any of her friends about the wedding or the baby and in those days, you did as you were told! We went and bought the wedding ring for 10 guineas. Now another hurdle to get over as we have to find somewhere to live a bit quickly. Fortunately, my sister Ann and her husband Brian came to the rescue!! They let us move in with them in a 2-bedroom flat at 13, College Road. We got married on a very snowy Monday, the 26th February 1962 at Epsom Registry Office, although Elaine's mum said she wouldn't go, in the end she did. It was just a very small affair and my mum did some sandwiches. Pat picked Elaine up and it was touch and go as to whether they would make it with the thick snow. We did get our white wedding after all! We couldn't wait to get away on a train to London for our 3-night honeymoon. Pat took us to the station and we were on our way and very happy. Ann booked the hotel for us, but unfortunately it was not a very good one. It was The Strand Palace Hotel with no bathroom, but we did really enjoy it and had a lovely time.

After the month in the small flat we all moved to 1, Bridge Road in Epsom, a large house with 2 kitchens. Ann and Brian lived downstairs and we lived upstairs (apart from our kitchen). It was a very cold, old house so it was very hard to keep warm. We had icicles inside the windows and had to have a paraffin heater in our bedroom for warmth and during that winter used to all sit in Ann and Brian's kitchen with the oven on with the door open to keep warm. We never used our living room in the winter as it was so very large. Sharing the rent and bills meant we could afford to live there. I sold Pat my half share in the car and all he could afford to give me was £100, but it helped to pay for the wedding and down payment for hire purchase for our essential furniture. Also, we did have a few wedding presents. Elaine had to stop work soon after as she had high blood pressure and the journey (standing nearly all the time) was doing her no good. But then she did get some maternity money which helped. I was so very fortunate to be able to be with Elaine during her labour as this was really unheard of in those days, such an experience I will never forget, I wouldn't have missed it for the world. Stephen Paul was born on 10th July 1962 and weighed 7lbs 6oz, and he was just so beautiful and much loved by everyone. His name for me was special as it was also a good sprinter's name who was trained by Atty Persse at Stockbridge. During those days you were kept in hospital for 10 days after the birth, and her mum was besotted with Stephen, but it didn't change her attitude to me at all. I was not welcome by her for a few years, so I used to drop Elaine off to visit with Stephen and collect her before stables. I was fortunate that I had the work's van that I could use during the afternoons when I was home and not racing. Being home of an afternoon was great as I could see much more of Stephen during the day.

I formed a friendship with someone Wally knew called Ron Spackman, he was a settler for an Epsom bookmakers. He was a very generous man to me as I very often gave him a winner, so he used to give me a share of his winnings. He was a single chap who lived with a lovely old lady in Fir Tree Road Epsom. Over the years we got very friendly consequently this extra money all helped us a lot and we did have quite a few winners in 1962.

The winter of 62/63 was really bad, so much snow, I used to have to dig the minivan out every morning before I could start it, but amazingly it started every time! I used to leave it on the Downs by The Rubbing House as the snow was too deep to drive down to Langley Vale. I always managed to get to work as the horses needed seeing to each day. When we arrived at work, before we could get to the horses, we had to dig the snow out which was about 4 foot deep against the doors. Our house was really so very cold, freezing in fact, but it really made Stephen a hardy little lad. We spent our 1st Christmas as a family in Bridge Road along with mum, Wally and Noreen and Uncle Pat, and they supplied all the food of course! In the early spring Brian said to me that they wanted to 'move on' (obviously finding it hard to pay their contribution of the rent). The very next day he came and told us about a house in Ashtead up for rent. I went to see the owner and Mrs Sirett vouched for me and we were told we could rent it.

At last we moved to a place of our own, 175 Craddocks Avenue, in April 1963. The lads who worked for Mr Wootton moved our furniture (such as it was) for us in a tractor and trailer driving this through Epsom town and this was illegal really! Bearing in mind that in those days Craddocks Avenue was a select area, so what the neighbours thought I don't know! When I went to give them a fiver, they didn't want to take it, but of course I made them as that was a real favour to us. Our rent was very expensive being £6 each week and on top of that £2 for rates and all I was bringing home now was £13 a week. There was no family allowance for the first child in those days. Elaine's mum had started to engage with me and they did spend Christmas with us and they helped by buying the food. We found out that Elaine was pregnant again in May 1963; we were very pleased of course, but not Elaine's mum! Elaine's Auntie Mary had come down from Sheffield around this time and when she went back it was decided that Elaine would take Stephen back with her to see all the relatives in Eckington. They went on the bus to Victoria and then got the coach up north. Having so many relatives in Eckington, Stephen really got spoilt with money, which was very handy as we could buy a lot of his clothes with this. In hindsight this was not a good time to do this with Elaine being in the very early stages of her pregnancy. Unfortunately, she had a miscarriage while up there, so very sad for us both.

1963 was another fairly good year for winners, for which we were thankful, but in the winter, Elaine decided she would do some housework jobs during the afternoons while I was home. These didn't last for long as again we found out Elaine was pregnant, so I managed to get some gardening jobs instead. That year we started having racing lads as lodgers, these lads worked for Jackie Sirett. We had a spare room and the £4 a week came in very handy, mind you we didn't like having them but needs must to pay the bills. We had a TV given to us which was great of an evening for us and being black and white it didn't need a license. The 1963/64 winter was better weather-wise, also having a boiler in the kitchen helped to dry off my clothes if I came home wet, Elaine hated the smell! I often used to take Elaine and Stephen to the yard when Jackie Sirett was away as Stephen loved it. That summer Ron Spackman bought us a fridge, such a luxury for us.

Bryan Leyman left Sirett's in 1964 to go jumping.

Fortunately, Elaine had a trouble- free pregnancy, but due to having had high blood pressure with Stephen, they wanted her to have the baby in hospital again. We weren't very happy about that as she had to stay in for 8 days this time. Again, I stayed at hospital and it was just a 4- hour labour this time. We were blessed with our beautiful daughter Caron Jacqueline who weighed 6lb 10oz. In those days children were not allowed to visit which was so sad for both Elaine and Stephen. Elaine's mum stayed and looked after Stephen – bad move really as it didn't work out well! I did tell her to go home and that I would get my mum over, but she didn't want that of course, so she stayed until Elaine came home. You can imagine I was very pleased when Elaine finally came home and so was Stephen and now, we were a very happy family once more. While all this was happening, of course, we didn't have lodgers with us for a while. When things settled down, we started having lodgers again; none of them were any good really, just a real nuisance except for Bryan Leyman, our very last lodger and the best!

That summer was a moderate year for winners, the winters were worse for us financially due to the bigger heating bills. Now that we had 2 children, we were entitled to Family Allowance of 8 shillings per week collected from the post office every Tuesday. With this Elaine used to buy the dinners from Tuesday to Friday when it was pay day! In 1964 Wendy Bentley came to us along with another girl called Denise (nickname Granny). When Wendy's dad and Granny's mum took the girls for the interview with Jackie apparently Granny's mum asked Jackie what prospects there were for her daughter (she was a bit of a snob!) So, Jackie said "No prospects for girls!" and to this Granny's mum said "What do you employ them for then?" Now this is unbelievable what he said! He said "To keep the lads happy" and was laughing all the time when he said it. So,

Granny's mum wasn't keen for her to work there and in effect told her she should move out of the family home. They ended up both working for us and Granny went to live with Wendy and her mum and dad for 6 years. Of all the girls I have had any dealings with in racing Wendy was the best, such a very efficient stable girl, I have never seen any better and what's more she could also ride really well. Johnny Gilbert, a marvellous jockey over hurdles, had a daughter called Ann who wanted to work in racing. He came and had a word with me telling me he wouldn't send her to anyone else as I would look after her. She was with us for about a year and then Johnny started the Racing School at Goodwood so she went with him. Later on, going to Newmarket starting another one which became a big concern and is still going strong today. Ann went on to marry Ray Cochrane, the Derby winning jockey, and many years later we met them both at a New Year's Eve dance on Newmarket Race Course. They were a lovely couple who wanted to talk to both Elaine and I. On that evening Ann said to me not to ever think of going back into racing because it would not be "me" as she said they didn't do it my way anymore!!

I used to get Christmas boxes from quite a few of the owners in the way of money, so all very gratefully received and used for Christmas presents for both Stephen and Caron. Christmas Eve 1964 and Elaine had her 21st little party at home, her mum helped with doing the food. Well, I went to pick Ron up early evening and Lord Roseberry had given me a really good cigar. Ron wasn't ready and there was a great fire burning in the living room so I decided to light up, not a good move as I hadn't had a lot to eat! I was very ill driving home and ended up going to bed, that is until Robin Douglas (another racing pal) arrived and made me a port and brandy and then I was as right as rain. All of this did really spoil it all for Elaine though.

Into 1965 and we were just jogging along financially. Every 2 weeks on my Sunday afternoon off I was able to use the works van, so we used to either go to Box Hill, Headley Heath or Epsom Downs taking a picnic which we loved. In the summer months we would take a drive down the coast and have a picnic and ice creams! I was allowed just 1 week day holiday each year – just Monday to Friday and it had to be taken during a slack time. As time went on, I used to get a whole Sunday off - heaven! Summer 1965 and we had our first holiday in our friend Joan Bartholomew's mum's caravan at Bracklesham Bay. She never charged us as Elaine used to look after Joan's son, Gary, occasionally while Joan worked in the shop, although Joan always bought us some sausages. In the September I managed to get Monday to Friday off and John Carter took and collected us, as I was not allowed the work's van to go away in! John was very generous to Stephen and Caron giving them enough pocket money for the week. We all really enjoyed being away, good weather and Stephen and Caron loved the beach. When I returned to work George (our head lad at home) had in fact left and I was offered his job if I wanted it. Elaine and I discussed this and decided it would be better if I took it. Lord Roseberry had always sent us some nice horses in the 1st year having 14 winners, but now being 1965, he was sending most of them to private trainer, Jack Jarvis at Newmarket. We did have Mr Buchanan and Mr Stanthorpe Joel who had a few winners, but mostly it was private owners.

HEAD LAD AT HOME

Therefore, in the end I decided to take the job of Head Lad at home, which meant I was the yard manager. When I accepted Jackie asked me did I want to have the same as he gave George for a winner i.e., £15 or leave it up to him if he had a nice touch. I agreed with the latter, but on reflection it was bad judgement. The 1st horse that won was 'Resistance' and Jackie gave me £30 for the next winner I got £25 and it finally went down to £10 per winner. From the owners I would only get what they wanted to give me, sometimes good but more often than not bad. However, I did have £2 more each week for this job and I was busier what with making the mash twice a week in the copper clipping all the horses on my own as Jackie still only employed boys. I used to administer medication i.e., balling the horses, either Cupiss or physic balls. For both of these extra jobs I never got paid any more money of course. When I balled the horses, they were held for me and being left- handed, the way I did this was to get the horses tongue in my right hand and the ball in my left. On my left hand I had a leather mitten to save me from getting cut on the back molars. This ball had been warmed up, either on the copper or in my pocket. I followed the roof of the mouth with the ball right over into the gullet and then pushed it down. When I did this, I would jerk the head up quickly so they couldn't cough it up. Then I would put my hand in my pocket and pull out a little bit of grass to give to the horse and while they chewed it, I would watch it go down their throat. I used to do this for other trainers also and got paid about £2 each horse and sometimes more. There was no one else that I knew of in Epsom who could do this except Billy Crump, who was head lad for Wallington, but had since died. I have heard of others doing it, but to my knowledge, they did it with a 12" piece of hose pipe, this was not ideal as it could easily fall out. Consequently, Jackie rarely needed a vet and if he did the vet would tell me what to do and I only had to be shown once then I could do it next time.

I used to break all the yearlings in, just getting one of the boys to chase them to keep going on a lunge. When the yearling was ready to ride away, I would put one of the boys on it. Owners used to look around some evenings and would generally leave a present for both myself and the lad who did the horse. A few perks, but not enough to make up for the poor wage for the long working week. This all brings back what my Gran used to say to me when I first started in racing. I used to go home and say to her that the owners have looked around. So she asked, "Well did they give you a present then?" I said, "No," so she told me what to say the next time they came round. "If you find, when you get home, that you have lost your purse, just remember you never pulled it out here." All this said I really did enjoy all my time working with horses.

It was around this time that Elaine had put our name down for a council house in both Epsom and Leatherhead, but no chance we were told.

Christmas was good as always, all the relatives spoilt Stephen and Caron, and with my presents from the owners we always managed to buy them something from us. Elaine's mum and dad always came to us for Christmas which helped with the food, also spoiling Stephen and Caron as well.

1965 and 1966 there wasn't a lot going on as far as winners were concerned. We did have various lads as lodgers to help the money worries out, but, unfortunately, some of the lads were not very nice to have at all, but the best of it was they went to bed early, in fact soon after their evening meal. I was still doing my gardening jobs and Elaine doing housework jobs. When Arthur and Heather got married, he gave his notice to Jackie as he started training. I helped him out by giving him 3 saddles and 2 bridals. During his first winter of training, I also used to go up to the yard near Reigate some afternoons and clip his jumpers and did this off my own back out of fondness for Heather. Bryan went to work for Arthur and came to lodge with us. Of course, we now needed another Travelling Head Lad and Graham Jennings, who had served part of his apprenticeship with Jackie, took on the job. Again, Graham was another good Travelling Head Lad, but he didn't stay long!

In1967 Elaine decided that she would get an afternoon job, as there were jobs going at PTS betting office in Leatherhead and the hours were good and fitted in well. 1pm to 5pm weekdays and 12 noon to 5pm on Saturdays with one day off in the week. I would drop Elaine off each day and then take Stephen and Caron home and go back again before stables to drop them off at Elaine's mum and dad's for about an hour and a half. Now things were looking up for us financially at last! Stephen started at Greville School in Ashtead in September 1967 and settled in very well coming out at 3pm which was just right for me to pick him up. Some days I would take Stephen up the yard (only when Jackie was racing of course) Stephen loved it, and Caron loved being on her own with her Nan. When I took Stephen up the yard, I would put him on the back of a horse called 'Steel Don' (strangely he was also 5 years' old). After a while of doing this, I would put the tack on 'Steel Don' and put Stephen on him and lead him around the yard and Stephen had no fear at all. Because of that I got rather complacent and used to leave him in the stable on his back when he was walking around his box, eating hay and looking over the stable door. On reflection I was a little silly to do this, but because he had no fear, I carried on doing it until one day one of the apprentices came and told me that Stephen had fallen off in the box onto the straw!! He didn't hurt himself and I put him back on again as this is what he wanted. This horse was so quiet that I now feel that one of the apprentices may have frightened him.

October 1967 and we were both very concerned about the fact that we could be having another baby, as lovely as it was, we just couldn't afford another one!! When it was confirmed, Elaine decided she would have to really badger the councils about a house. We had very little luck to begin with.

As per usual Christmas was good even though we gave Elaine's mum and dad the news about another baby. 1968 and Elaine worked for as long as she could, still badgering the councils, and low and behold we were offered a council house in Ashtead at the beginning of the week and then offered one in Epsom the end of the same week! Seeing as Stephen was enjoying his school and we both really didn't want to move to Epsom, we decided on the Ashtead one. In the April of 1968 we moved to 24, Berry Meade, Ashtead. Our landlord at Craddocks Avenue was very sad to see us go as we had been really good tenants, he never had any problems with us. We knew that as much as having a third baby was not on the cards it did us a good favour. We feel sure we would never have got another house otherwise, so good on you Gavin! Now we saw a difference financially, even though Elaine gave up work. Instead of paying £8 rent and £2 rates each week, we were paying £2 18 shillings each week and that was for rent and water rates! So, it was about £3 each week for rent, rates and water which was a huge difference. Again, we moved ourselves with the help of Den King (Elaine's cousin's husband) and Graham Jennings. We remained good friends with Graham and his wife Beryl. The décor at 24 was horrendous, bright orange paint nearly everywhere (even the toilet cistern). We always maintain that the chap before us must have had a job lot from the council seeing as he worked for them. So, Lionel and I started decorating and by the time Gavin was born our bedroom, along with the bathroom were all decorated. The garden was very long, mainly to lawn, but I got that sorted even though the couple who had the house before had buried so much stuff in the garden including an iron bedstead! When we moved in there wasn't one light bulb or curtain track, so we had to start from scratch. Uncle Pat said we could buy his car from him for £50 which we did and paid him back when I had a couple of winners. He went on tell me that he had never been paid back so promptly from anyone in the family before. This car didn't last long at all, had so much wrong with it so not a good buy at all. In May 1968, just a few weeks after we moved, Stephen became very ill, he was up all night with very bad diarrhoea and had been poorly for a few days prior to this. Elaine called Dr Smith who told us to just give him sips of water. Because Stephen never complained when he was ill, we never realised how bad he was and should not have been happy with the Doctor treating him over the phone. What we didn't realise was that he was developing pneumonia and was hallucinating. This was at the weekend and I had arranged to take our furniture that we no longer wanted down to Ann and Brian in Bognor. I had borrowed a van from a friend so I really wanted to get it done, in hindsight I should never had done that. Elaine rang Dr Smith after we had left who came out and called an ambulance (flashing lights and sirens going all the way). Elaine had left a note for me on the door to tell me what had happened (Ann and Brian had no phone) and what hospital they had gone to. Diagnosis was that Stephen had gastro enteritis plus pneumonia and was extremely poorly. He was taken to St Mary's Children's Hospital in Carshalton, and as soon as I got home with Caron, we made our way there. Such a worrying time for us both especially as Caron also got it a few days later (thankfully not as bad as Stephen) but she ended up in hospital also! They both had to be in isolation rooms and we had to cap and gown up each time we went in their rooms. In those days parents never stayed with their children overnight so I took Elaine there every day and then went on to work for a few hours before going back again. Caron came out of hospital before Stephen which was good news. Not one of the doctors ever thought that Stephen would survive and he was there for a few weeks. During this time Elaine was experiencing tummy pains and our doctor was concerned that she would lose the baby. Of course, the pains were due to her not eating or sleeping. When Stephen finally came out of hospital all of the doctors and nurses lined up to shake his hand as they felt it was a miracle he had survived. Of course, Stephen being Stephen took it all in his stride and it wasn't long before he was back at school fighting fit!

Life then settled down once more and I could get some more decorating done and we could look forward to another baby being born, this time at home. So, Elaine had our son Gavin Stewart at home with just a midwife present on Sunday 23rd June 1968. This midwife was Irish and was really lovely, chatting to me all the time about 'Arkle' the Gold Cup winner. We were meant to have a trainee midwife present but our midwife cancelled her when she couldn't hear a heartbeat. Such a really good midwife as never once did she let on that she was concerned we would have a still birth. Gavin was born in distress so the midwife called for a doctor from our practice to come out and he arrived just after the birth and was happy with everything. Of course, yet again I ended up receiving the third degree from Elaine's mum about never having another baby! This time I wasn't going to have her looking after things at home while Elaine was in bed so we had a wonderful home help come in each morning to do all the washing and ironing and keep things tidy and cook the dinner.

On 3rd August 1968 Elaine's friend Maureen married Sandy at Leatherhead Parish Church and Caron was bridesmaid. Caron was so excited and looked beautiful and Maureen of course looked stunning. Stephen enjoyed handing Maureen a horseshoe from the horse Easy to Love.

That year was a very lean year regarding winners as Jackie never bought any good horses. We were enjoying living in

Berry Meade even though it was such a small house with three children. 1968 and 69 were lean years as far as winners were concerned, so we were both undecided about where I should go from here. When lo and behold, Graham Jennings had started working at Heathrow airport and said if I wanted, he would get me an application form. So, I gave my notice into Jackie! Stanley Wootton found out and sent for me. He told me that he couldn't have a chap like me leaving racing, so would I work for him? He gave me a week to make my mind up so I thought about this long and hard and decided I would put a couple of conditions to him. Saturday lunch time at 12 noon he walked into the yard. "Well, my boy what have you decided to do?" I told him I had conditions with the job. "What are they, my boy?" he said, no one ever gave Stanley conditions. First one I said was that I would need my weekends off and the second one was to raise my wages by £2 per week. He looked at me and said "I hope you get what you want" and turned and walked away. This man was one of the biggest names in racing, a millionaire who owned half of Epsom and had many, many interests over the racing world. So much for him saying to people years before that I was the best! I was however very pleased to leave it all behind me as I always said I would leave racing before I was 40.

LIFE AFTER RACING

Graham got me an application form to work for British European Airways, but unfortunately for me there were no vacancies at that time. They did advise me to apply at a later date, so I needed to find a job in the meantime. At that time Dave Wager (another racing mate who had his own business) wanted someone to help him out. I did for a short while, but it didn't work out and nearly broke our friendship up, so I left and found a job window cleaning in Dorking at Lawrence and Tester. I really enjoyed it as they were a good bunch of lads. We used to travel all over the place window cleaning for large firms and hospitals and the pay was quite good. It was at this time I discovered Jackie Sirett gave up training, coincidentally only one year after I left him!! In 1970 I rented an allotment in Leatherhead which was in a bad state. I managed tidy it up and ended up growing lovely vegetables and soft fruit, shortly after I got a second one so I was kept very busy in my spare time. In 1971 I again applied to BEA (which was later to become British Airways) and managed to get a job as a ramp worker working on the tarmac for the cleaning and handling section. After a few months I became a driver then after that became a ramp worker on water section again as a driver. After 2 years I became ramp worker 1 – this meant I was a leading hand with my own crew. Each time I earnt more money of course which all helped. It was all shift work but I was used to this from my racing days. However, these shifts were much better as I would work 4 days on and have 3 days off or 3 days on and have 2 days off. The shift pattern was early mornings, late afternoons or nights and nights only came around every 7 weeks. There was always lots of overtime which I used to do as well. At last, we could afford to get a decent car, all the bangers we did have kept breaking down on me and for that journey I needed something more reliable. I will never forget Concord and its first training flight at Heathrow. My crew and I heard it was in so we all decided after we finished our job to go and see if we could have a look around it. There didn't seem to be any room on it at all compared to the jumbo jets we were used to, and how the pilot managed to get in the cockpit I will never know. The plane was a little disappointing at first and the noise when it took off was unbearable. I had never seen anything like it before or since and I never thought it would be in service for as long as it was. However, it was an incredible piece of technology but the expense was so great I feel sure this was the reason for its downfall. We used to play cards a lot during our break time, mostly poker, just for small stakes. One day they organised a crib contest taking in all of the shifts and eliminating them, there being 4 shifts in all with 10 crew to a shift. I knew I was a decent crib player having played with John Carter. We all paid £1 entrance fee with prizes for 1st, 2nd and 3rd at the end. Obviously, I was a bit rusty, but believe it or not I got to the final making a lot of mistakes in the final but I still won. The chap I beat had all the decent cards and he did his nut telling me I couldn't play the game – but I knew the proof of the pudding as they say! The funny thing was I was fed up with the game by the time I reached the final; this is how I always felt playing cards. I made a good friend called Ken Ward there and we were still in contact with each other until he passed away. Also, towards the end of my time at Heathrow I made another good friend called Harry Kew, poor Harry has since died but we are still in touch with his wife who now lives in Wakefield. Some of the chaps there used to play tricks on their crew, especially when they were bored waiting for the aircraft to be ready to clean. Quite regularly one of the tricks that a couple of them played always happened first thing in the morning when the new shift started. Firstly, we would make a cup of tea and sit down and read the paper. One of the workers used to crawl along the ground with his cigarette lighter and set light to the bottom of the paper of one of the unsuspecting lads. He would then crawl back very quickly and start reading his own paper again. Well, the paper would flare up all of a sudden and you can imagine the language that was used! This never happened to me as I never bought a paper! During my time at Heathrow, I had several gardening jobs I did on my days off and the first year I also painted five houses outside, so was always kept busy what with the allotments as well.

When Stephen and Gavin were aged 10 and 4, I would take them up to Wendy at Tadworth who had worked for Jackie. After leaving Jackie she went back to her previous job and also had a couple of ponies that she let them ride. Both Stephen and Gavin really enjoyed riding her ponies.

In 1973 we moved to a new council house in Leatherhead as we already knew Berry Meade was only temporary because it wasn't big enough for 3 children. Again, Graham and Den helped us move in. By now Elaine was working for an agency for five hours a day enabling her to be home for the children after school. Later as the children got older, she changed to working full time for Decca Survey in Leatherhead until being made redundant in 1986.I worked at Heathrow until 1982 when they were offering good redundancy payments and a company pension. At the time all of our electrical appliances had worn out, so now we had the money to replace them all. It was a bit more difficult getting another job this time, but I managed to get one working for Michael's coach service in Sutton driving children with physical or learning needs to school and back. There was one round I wasn't keen on along The Roundshaw Estate in Croydon. Funnily enough no other driver wanted to do it either. Fortunately for me I did have a lovely escort by the name of Chris, an Irish lady who became a great friend of both of ours. I used to do three school runs and during my second year I received another contract for a nursery just outside Sutton. Some of these children were disabled; the others came from broken homes etc. When it was getting near Christmas the lady in charge asked me if I would dress up as Santa Claus for the children. Chris was an expert dressmaker and made my outfit and I was really looking forward to doing this for the children. I took a cassette player along and played Christmas songs and walked into the classroom singing and banging on the walls and shouting, "ho ho ho." I had my sack of presents supplied by the nursery and a grotto had been made for me. The children came to me one by one and sat on my knee (couldn't do that nowadays!) Of course, I asked them what they wanted and asked if they had been good. All of the children loved it and it made my Christmas making all those children so happy. That year I had so many Christmas cards from the children and their parents.

Once I left racing, we lost touch with Heather Pitt but in 1984 she bought South Hatch Racing Club in Epsom. It opened in 1985 and at that time we were unaware of it and it was only when Bryan and his wife Lin came to us one weekend that we all decided to book a table and go and surprise Heather. She was in her usual place, in the kitchen, we were told. So, we asked one of the waitresses to ask her to come and see us (not telling her who we were). As you can imagine Heather was amazed to see Bryan and us. It was a real trip down memory lane and the food was spectacular. As luck would have it, I left my jacket there and Heather rang us up in the morning to ask if it was mine or Bryan's. This was another chance for us to meet up and Elaine and I decided to join the club. We had so many wonderful celebrations there and always had a great time. During the 1990's Heather used to arrange a tea party for all the ex-jockeys and all of them really enjoyed this having a good chat to all their old mates. As usual Heather laid on a good spread and this happened about three times a year. Heather arranged for an old friend of hers, called Joy, to bring her piano and play all the old songs for us so we all could have a good sing song and a dance. When sadly Heather passed away Wendy, her lovely daughter, carried on doing these tea parties for us all. Both Heather and Wendy really enjoyed the jockey's banter and all of us ex-jockeys and wives were really blessed to have Heather and then Wendy do this for us. Looking back, we would never have got together otherwise; they were two very special people in our lives. As a bonus, by getting to know Heather again, we were brought more blessings by the way of Allan and Shirley Harris. Allan Harris had been a great footballer in his day. Heather rang me and said she didn't know whether she had done the right thing but she had put my name forward as a gardener for them both. I did say that I was very busy but would go and see them. I went and spoke to Allan and he said that they only needed me for an hour a week! Well, if you could see the garden, you would know that was not enough time. I told him that I couldn't do much in an hour but how about 3 hours. They were such a very special couple. I carried on doing this once we moved to Bognor for as long as I could, however we always remained such very good friends. Allan sadly passed away at the end of 2017, Elaine and I felt honoured to have known him like we did. Ken Ward who I worked with for many years told me what I thought was a funny story. He lived in the USA for a few years when he was young. He was conscripted into the army just before the Korean War. Ken went to fight in Korea and then came back for demob, because he had such a good time, he was going to miss all of the friends he made. He and his friends had to go in one by one to get their demob papers. Afterwards they were all chatting outside and they all told Ken they were going back into the army because they had such a good time. Ken thought to himself that he would do the same. When he returned outside, they were all having a good laugh as they hadn't signed on again at all. It all backfired on Ken!!

I left Michaels in 1986 and managed to get a job working for BT cleaning the offices in Weybridge. I started early in the morning and finished early in the afternoon. Later I was transferred to the Walton branch and did the same thing. Unbeknown to me this office was just over the fence from another old mate from racing Cliff Taylor and I never even knew. If I had known I would have popped in for lunch now and again. I would have continued with this job but in 1992 they sacked all of the staff over 60 but I did leave with a pension. During this time, I was still doing all of my gardening jobs, also helping Stephen doing night work jobs and really enjoying it. Caron met Steve when she was working in a pub in Bookham in 1983, they married in 1985. Both Elaine and I always classed Steve as our third son and both Stephen and Gavin had a great brother-in-law. In 1986 Elaine started working for Wood Harris Export Company, after having 3 months off up until our first grandchild Ryan Stephen was born in Poole in 1986 and 18 months later Chloe Antoinette, our first granddaughter was born. (This was the same day that my mum passed away also.) Stephen met Alison in 1989 and married in the summer of 1990. Their first child, a little girl, Amy Eloise was born at the end of that year. Then our third granddaughter Emily Alicia came along 2 years' later and then our fourth granddaughter Imogen Freya in 1997. Gavin met Cara in 1998 and married in 1999. This was the year that Elaine decided to take early retirement so that we could pay off our mortgage and move to Bognor.

We moved to a detached bungalow where we had 7 quality years. There was everything to do in the bungalow as it had been really let go, but we worked together indoors and got it all decorated. Steve used to come down regularly and clear out the garden and do all the heavy jobs for us. At the end of the same year Elaine's mum and dad moved to Henfield and really enjoyed living there. Stephen and Alison gave us our 2nd grandson in 2002, called Joshua Louis, so great for them to have a boy. Gavin and Cara had their first child Alfie Joseph in 2003, but unfortunately, he was stillborn, such a really sad time for all the family. Elaine's dad died early 2004 at the age of 89 but towards the end of that year Cara and Gavin had a baby girl whom they named Lily Frances. Their marriage broke down a year later and they were divorced in 2006. This year was a bad year all round, as Steve was diagnosed with terminal cancer and my sister Ann and her husband had a horrific car accident, Brian died the same day and Ann lasted 6 months. Also, in 2006 Elaine's mum passed away. It was decided that it would be better if we could move to be closer to Caron and Steve. So, we sold our bungalow in the spring of 2007 and rented a flat for a year in Horsham while we had a wonderful house built in Caron and Steve's Garden.

By this time, we had joined Racing Welfare having coffee mornings at The Epsom Club. Then in 2007 Elaine had a phone call from Sharon (who was in charge of Racing Welfare at the time) to say that Tony was to be awarded Lifetime in Racing Award. This was to be held at Brighton Racecourse (definitely not one of my favourites!) on May 30th. She asked Elaine to keep it a secret, but no way could she do that, she did say that we could invite all of our family, which we did. Well, the weather on the day couldn't have been worse, wind and rain and when that happens at Brighton you surely know it! None the more for that everyone had a great day, especially Steve. I was interviewed on the radio and had the first race named after me, The E.B.F. Tony Bowles Lifetime in Racing Maiden

Stakes. The winner was Sir Joshua Reynolds would you believe and ridden by an apprentice by the name of William Buick, who was later to become one of the country's top jockeys. We all had a few pennies on it. After the race Elaine was presented with a bouquet of flowers from John Akehurst and I received a bronze horse's head engraved. Just the two of us went into the private suite for champagne along with the trainer. Then back to the room where our family were for sandwiches and drinks. I did think it was rather embarrassing as every time I walked by the commentator he was saying, "Can you believe this man was riding in the 1940's?" A lovely day had by all in spite of the weather, with such special memories.

In 2008 we moved into our wonderful little house.

In the January of 2010 Steve passed away after having gone through such gruelling treatment for his cancer, he fought all the way. A wonderful man taken far too soon from his great family.

Not long after this sad time Chloe decided she would love to have a boxer dog, so they got a puppy and called him Revi. Such a wonderful dog and he was their salvation. Ryan was now in the army also going to Afghanistan, again another worrying time for the family.

In 2011 Elaine decided to email Johnjo O'Neill's P.A. at Jackdaw's Castle Training Establishment in Cheltenham to see if we could go and look around his yard as I had been talking about doing this. She did mention that it was for a special birthday present for me! Also, we wanted Joy and Cliff (our racing friends) to go with us. The young girl was very accommodating and invited us there for the day. At the time Joy and Cliff's son-in-law had an empty house in Cheltenham which he said we could stay in. We were all amazed when we got to the establishment early in the morning for breakfast, as a big buffet was laid on and the champagne was flowing. There were several owners there, and it was held in his hospitality suite. We then went to see the horses out exercise on the gallops. Johnjo was so very friendly to all of us and even wanted us to go racing at Cheltenham in the afternoon but we had made prior arrangements. After that we looked around the yard, which was just spectacular, 3 big yards with about 200 horses. We saw them swimming in the pool and then in the sauna. Then they went up the gallops, it was a real eye opener to me as I had never seen anything like this, of course, in my day. Johnjo asked me what I thought and I told him how well they all look also very happy and he said to me "So they should as this is a 5-star hotel!" and it surely was.

The next year Elaine decided to do this again with the Nigel Twiston-Davis yard, she again had a great response, but this yard comparing it to Johnjo's was the other extreme being like a farmyard compared with his, but he is very well liked and a good trainer with winners every day. No champagne or sandwiches here. Assistant trainer Carl Llewelyn, who rode a national winner, showed us around. Again, we stayed at Joy and Cliff's son-in-law.

In 2013 Caron made the decision to sell the property, so we also decided to move with her. That same year Gavin started courting Jo and they married in 2016 and now live in Littlehampton. We moved into a 6-bedroom new build in February 2014 to a village called Felpham, near Bognor so like déjà vu for us. In 2016 Amy married Steve, who she met while at Bath University and they live in a house in Dorking. Ryan is living with his partner Kirsty in a house in Southwater where he has worked so very hard on the property. Chloe had a baby boy called Reggie John on June 29th 2018, our first great grandchild. They live in Durrington. Imogen met her boyfriend, Marley in 2015. Ryan and Kirsty had their baby boy called Ralph Stephen Brown on May 18th 2020. Amy and Steve had Elijah Isaac on December 16th 2020. On December 9th 2021 Chloe had her 2nd baby boy Dennis Stephen– so we are building our own football team up! But on October 10th 2022 Amy and Steve had their lovely daughter called Elsie Maia.

Emily lives in Dudley with her partner Haydn.

In 2020 we moved to a 2-bedroom flat again in Felpham right near the seafront. Caron now lives in Elmer.

The Injured Jockey's Fund have been so very good to us over my twilight years and Lucy Charnock is our contact and is always there for us at the end of the phone helping in whatever way she can.

Katy is our contact at Racing Welfare and they are also very helpful.

Lifetime in Racing Award Brighton May 2007

Winner of my sponsored race was William Buck

Elaine and Tony 2020 at Leyton Court

Elaine

Gavin Bowles 1982

Cranleigh International Road Race

First youth to finish

Stephen
Paul,
Caron
and
Gavin
Bowles,
children
of
Tony
and
Elaine.
May
1972.

Stephen Caron and Gavin

1967 Stephen on Steel
Don

Wedding of Caron Bowles to Steve Brown

August 3rd 1985

Tony and Elaine Open Day

Tony

My Love
Our timeless memories will guide us through, my
life's complete thanks to you.

Elaine and Tony 26/2/1962

After wedding

My mum, Cecily Anne Bowles (Nee Kelly)

Mum was born at Holly Lodge on 29th May 1905. After her brother Billy died at a young age, she became the eldest of four children. Mum always went to good schools and was the favoured child. When she left school, her dad paid for her to be an apprentice in London to one of the finest seamstresses. She didn't like this job so told her dad she was very ill and had to come home. Consequently, she never finished her apprenticeship and Grandad lost all of his money! When she arrived home, she went to bed but soon recovered. This was when she started to hang about in her dad's pub, The Lisle Castle. She was the only one in the family to be brought up like a lady. Her sister Aunt Noreen used to have to clean the bar and Uncle Pat would be working in the orchard all day. Gran felt so sorry for Pat that she sent him away to be with friends in Epsom and he started work for the council. Mum never knew how to cook and I can never remember her cooking a meal however, my dad idolized her and she could do no wrong in his eyes. If ever Noreen showed my dad any clothes she had bought, my dad would always say that they would look better on Cecily! When Mum had her teeth taken out, as they were all crooked, and had false ones put in she sent Dad a photo and all he said was they looked so much better before. When Pat and Ann lived with Gran, Mum always used to cuddle me. When I used to come home from school, I was always hungry and Mum would be playing the piano and would tell me she was busy. While Dad was serving in the army during the war Mum had to get a job at a dry-cleaners in Epsom doing alterations and I remember her cycling there and back on an old rickety bike. If ever Mum was depressed in her life, it was usually because we had no money and she would take to her bed. In 1948 Mr Charlie Bell had some horses in Upper High Street; a man who had just left the army was looking after them before they went abroad. I used to go up there sometimes to help out. One day when Mum was passing by, she noticed him and asked me who he was. I told her he was Walter (Wally) Johnson. The next day Mum rode past on her bike and asked him if he could fix it for her as the chain had come off. The next day she introduced herself and asked him where he was living. He told her that he was living over one of the boxes in the yard and had his meals with a lady in Albert Road. Mum asked him if he would like to lodge with her and he was delighted. While I was away in Upavon this relationship progressed and mum said the neighbours were talking so what was he going to do about it? Mum wrote to me soon after explaining that they were going to get married. I went to the bank and drew out £50 and sent it to them as a present. In later years mum told me it was the best present they had ever had. The marriage never worked for either of them although they stayed together. Wally died many years before Mum passed away. Mum never bore a grudge against anyone and was always loyal to her family. She never interfered in my marriage but never wanted to baby sit the children. She loved all of her grandchildren but only wanted them for a short time to visit her. She used to love getting dressed up and go out and act like the lady she was brought up to be. She loved to talk and gossip about anything and everything and loved an argument especially with her sister Aunt Noreen!

Pat, Tony and Ann

Wedding of Mum and Dad 12/11/1927

Elaine and Tony at Dad's tombstone in Military

Cemetery in Bari 2014

SGT. LEONARD EDMOND COOPER BOWLES

2189725, Royal Engineer.

801 Road Construction Company.

Died on 18th June 1944 age 37.

Remembered with Honour Bari War Cemetery.

My dad, Leonard Edmund Cooper Bowles

My dad was born in Tonbridge on 6th October 1906. His mum Fanny Bowles was just 16 years old and working at Tonbridge Boys' School a very select high school for boarders. I think her job must have been cleaning the dormitories. There was a young male teacher who worked there and he came from a very good family. Obviously, he must have fancied Fanny and she took a shine to him as she ended up giving birth to my dad! This was all kept hush hush seeing as he came from such a high-class family. They gave Fanny a lump sum of money to keep her quiet about who the father was. I am not sure whether he would have stood by her or not but I don't think he had much say in the matter. A few years later Fanny was offered another amount of money but refused to take it. Dad never knew who his father was however, I have always wondered whether the Cooper in his name was his dad's surname. This was sometimes the case years ago; his name could even have been Edmund Cooper. Dad was brought up by his maternal grandma and her partner who she called her husband. In fact, her real husband had left her years before when she was living in Tonbridge. Dad's real grandad Jesse Bowles worked near London and only came home at weekends. One weekend he came home to find his wife in bed with the lodger called Mr Jones. Jesse packed his bags and left. Gran had 5 children with Jesse the eldest being Fanny and she had 3 more children with Mr Jones. I never heard from or saw Fanny but mum did take us down to see granny who we called Berry Gran. This was during the war. Dad hated being brought up with his step aunts who were more or less the same age as him. When Fanny did get married to a man called Mr Buss, who was from Tonbridge, she of course wanted dad back with them so he did go. Berry Gran then found out that Mr Buss was abusing Dad so she went and had a row with Fanny and him and brought Dad back to live with her all very upsetting for him. Dad went to the local village school and by all accounts was a very bright child; he sang in the choir and ended up serving his time in the building trade eventually becoming a foreman. When he met my mum, I think he was the foreman of a chalk works nearby. My dad was the greatest dad anyone could have; there was no one else like him. It is so sad that when we were all born during the 30s, they were the slump years and he had to travel miles to get work. Dad would cycle off first thing in the morning and would come home when we were all in bed. Then we had to move house many times following his work around. I remember moving to a place called West Hall it was a flat overlooking a railway station and it took ages to get used to the noise of the trains. These were hard times for my dad and I can remember mum pawning her engagement ring to get some money together. The grand piano was given to Mum by Gran as a wedding present but in later years mum sold it to get an upright piano. This would have been cheaper so she would have had money left over to buy food. During the 30s we moved many times eventually ending up at 71 College Road Epsom in 1939. By this time dad had a permanent job with the council, then, of course, war broke out and dad signed up. I said goodbye to him in early 1940 on West Ewell station and never saw him again. I feel so sad that I never knew my dad when I was older. The letters he would write to me always said we would work together once the war was over. Having no dad at home I had to choose something I could do and being so tiny of course I chose to go into racing.

My Grandad Joseph Kelly

Joseph Kelly started work, or rather signed his apprenticeship papers in 1892 with Alec Taylor. Alec Taylor trained at Manton near Marlborough in Wiltshire. This was one of the biggest training establishments in the country. One day when he was very young, he and his brother, who also worked there, decided to run away. They only made it a mile before they heard the dinner bell ring so

Grandad went back but his brother continued going and never returned. During Grandad's apprenticeship the staff would sleep in the lofts above the horses inside a dormitory and he used to say that his life then was very hard. They were allowed a cup of tea once a year at Christmas and the rest of the time drank watered down ale. One day one of the paid lads threw one of the young boys down the stairs and killed him. This was all covered up as no one cared much in those days. It was always a case of looking after yourself. Grandad rode 14 winners as an apprentice not a bad return at all in those days. When he finished his apprenticeship, he made his way to Epsom and started training when he was only 21 years old and this is when he met my gran. He started with a few horses at a yard called Prime Lodge in Ashley Road. When he married Gran, he moved to a small yard and cottage at the top of Downs Road. From there he moved to Holly Lodge in Kingswood and there they lived until a bigger house was built with more stables. They had their first child there, a boy called Billy but he died when he was very young and is buried in the cemetery there. A further 3 children Dorothy, Cecily and Patrick were all born at Holly Lodge. They must have been there quite a few years before moving back to Epsom. This time they moved to Downs House which was next to The Derby Arms Pub. It changed its name to Derby Arms

Stable then Downs Stable, where their youngest daughter, Noreen was born. In 1912 they moved to Holme House Bishops Cleeve, Cheltenham. He bought this property from a Gloucestershire cricketer and it's still there today a lovely large house and in those days had a lot of stables in the yard. Elaine and I have been there to visit and look around. Then came the First World War and he had to go off to France and fight. He had to find different trainers to look after his horses until he returned. Grandad was at Ypres in Belgium and was up to his neck in mud one day trying to get the gun carriage horses to move. Low and behold a high-ranking officer recognized him from racing and shouted, "Joe Kelly, what on earth are you doing there, you shouldn't be out here," it was one of his owners. While Grandad was in Belgium all 4 of his children contracted diphtheria and were taken to the local cottage hospital in a black carriage with all the blinds down. This was a very sad day for my gran; poor Dorothy was coughing and being sick all night and had passed away by the morning. The other 3 children all recovered. When he returned from the war, he decided they should move to Ireland to train on The Curragh in a huge training facility. This was all during the troubles and he wasn't there long as Sinn Fein gave him a week to leave the country. He was a newcomer and not wanted. He had taken Gran's 2 brothers with him Albert and Walter they worked in the yard and were both very good golfers. Walter stayed in Ireland and married a local girl and became a professional golfer and stayed there all his life having one daughter. On returning to England Grandad went to Kent as one of his owners was a farmer and had many orchards there. He built a yard and laid out gallops and had much success; so much so he bought a pub called The Lisle Castle. Gran ran the pub which was about 5 miles away from the yard and it was here that Mum met Dad. After Mum left Lisle Castle, Grandad went back to Epsom and bought 71 College Road. He sold the pub so that Gran and Noreen could move to Epsom. Of course, Uncle Pat was already in Epsom in lodgings and working for the council and then when he married Jessie, he bought 69 College Road. Grandad stayed training in Kent just coming home at weekends. As far as I am aware he finished training in 1938. He was not a big trainer but was very shrewd and successful. He was a very hard man both at work and at home. Many people disliked him. Grandad never used to talk to me, he only ever grunted except the first time he put me on a horse. Even then he shouted at me and waved his arms around never telling me how to ride at all. The only real information I received about my Grandad was from my Gran.

My Gran Edith Kelly

I was always very close and fond of my gran. She came from a large family of 7 children and had an elder sister and 5 brothers. Three of her brothers were killed during the First World War I never knew their names. I knew Albert and Walter and her sister Alma but I always called her Auntie Page. She was a matron and always wanted to be the boss! When she fell ill, she came to stay with Gran and died in the room upstairs. Gran came from a small village in Norfolk called Holme by the Sea near Hunstanton. Her mother was just 35 when she died and her father married again. Gran always told me her step mother was fine until she had her own daughters. Later on in life they all used to visit gran and I always remember them being very nice. I think that with so many in the family living in a small cottage some of the children used to stay with relatives close by in the village. When I looked at the census, I discovered that Gran was living with a younger brother somewhere else. Elaine and I have visited the cottage and it was a very small place. Gran left home to go into service at the age of 14. She went to Epsom and worked in a kitchen in a large house. She told me the work was fine but the people she worked with were difficult. She must have met grandad when she was about 19 and they married when she was 21 (pregnant). When they moved into the cottage, she contracted diphtheria which she always put down to cleaning the outside drains. When they lived at Holly Lodge, she used to do her shopping in Epsom and one of the apprentices would drive the pony and trap. She told me it was hard living in a little lodge while the house was being built as there were no conveniences. Gran told me that Grandad was very hard on his apprentices and she saved them many a good hiding! Grandad was of the opinion that he learned the hard way and why shouldn't they? Years later while at College Road two of the old apprentices used to come to the house to talk to her at the back gate. They never forgot her kindness of 40 years previous. Gran told me that when they were in Ireland, she once heard guns firing during the night where Sinn Fein had pulled some unlucky person out of their bed and shot them. When they moved from Holly Lodge to Downs House grandad started to change and became grumpier. Grandad used to con owners into playing golf for money against Gran's brothers. Grandad always ended up winning the money. He probably gave her brothers a drink out of it. He used to go to a private club in London now and again and play cards. While lodging at 71 College Road, Gran used to save money, put it into savings and give me 2 shillings a week. She ended up saving about £100 for me and kept the book.

Gran never took any keep from me she just saved it. I used to do Gran's shopping for a pint of Guinness and 5 Weights cigarettes. She would have to stay in the kitchen with her glass and her cigarette because it would have upset "grumpy Joe" if she was in the living room with him in there. I used to feel awful that she had to do this. I was with gran for over 2 years and grew very close to her. She used to love me brushing her hair she would sit for ages while I brushed it almost making her fall asleep. She had her son Patrick living next door with Jesse and their daughter Janet. Gran would baby sit for her so Janet spent a lot of time with gran as well. Noreen was living with Gran and Grandad as she never left home. Grandad used to sleep in the front room upstairs and gran and Noreen in the back bedroom together. Gran was a good- looking woman when she was younger with a trim figure but once they bought the pub, she put on a lot of weight which didn't suit her at all.

**Joseph Kelly
1878-1961**

Gran

**Edith Elizabeth Kelly
1881-1954
Nee Callaby**

Gran and Grandad

HOLME HOUSE CHELTENHAM 1913

The Main House

Holy Lodge, Kingswood

Gran and Grandad

1905

> Veteran trainer Joe Kelly (remember Battleaxe?) entertained us with interesting memories of the long ago. Joe is now 77 years old, and recalled the days when the famous American jockeys Milton Henry and Danny Maher used to ride his horses.

Battleaxe

Lisle Castle Chalk Kent - Gran and Granddad's Pub Gran kept the pub and he trained

Conclusion

As I have said before I have always wondered why on earth my grandad didn't put me with a decent trainer, one who knew how to make jockeys (he definitely knew them all!) and there were quite a few around. I was the only one in the family who was interested in being in horse racing, but then my grandad was a very strange man!!

I must have broken in about 100 or more yearlings (just using a few select apprentices to ride them away) and these were Bryan Leyman, Mick Gillespie and Mick Haines. I clipped over 100 horses and administered medication to many of them. Only one horse (a mare of Stanley Wootton's) was any trouble and I knew this as soon as I went in the box. She knew every trick in the book to stop me getting the medicine ball down her! Serving an apprenticeship in racing just after the Second World War, as I did, was very hard on apprentices as all the jockeys were coming home from the war to ride again and in those days the apprentices got pushed out of the way. A lot of the race tracks that had been lying idle during the war years were opening up again.

Racing wasn't as closely watched as it is today and things happened in races that would never happen nowadays. 9

out of 10 apprentices would be intimidated by the older jockeys especially if it looked like they would beat them! My teenage riding years, although not reaching any dizzy heights, were very special to me. Being part of the racing community and working with horses was something I always had a huge passion for and loved. I know that if the money had been better, with every other weekend off I would never have left when I did. It was not a job for a family man in those days with working 7 days a week for such low wages, and holidays having to be taken out of season.

The biggest highlight in my racing life was during 1953 when I met and chatted to Charlie Grey. He talked to me about his experiences riding alongside Fred Archer during the 19th Century. Not many people of my era would have had this opportunity to speak with someone who had so many stories to tell. Of all the jockeys I rode alongside the one person who stands out head and shoulders above them all was Sir Gordon Richards. He was a true gentleman who gave me good advice, the likes of which I had never had before.

I also loved my two years in the army as it meant I was still working with horses although on reflection I wish I had the opportunity to go into the parachute regiment. Travelling horses abroad was a real experience for me in those days, something I would never have wanted to miss.

On reflection I also enjoyed my time at Heathrow airport, the people I worked with there were also a great bunch of lads and we always had a good laugh. Twelve years at the airport was enough for me though with all the travelling and shift work, again not a job for a family man. The bonus of working at the airport was the 1 free flight a year, being stand by, which we always used to visit Elaine's brother in Vancouver, meaning we had no hotels to pay neither. We could also have as many stand by 90% flights and firm booking 80% flights. The first 90% we had was also Elaine's first flight and we went to Jersey with Beryl and Graham Jennings for the weekend. The bed and breakfast we had was the one that the majority of the airline staff used and it was very good. We had a great weekend. The next time we went we took Stephen, Caron and Gavin and used the same bed and breakfast going at October half term as it was less busy to use stand by. At this time in our marriage, we would never have been able to afford these holidays without this perk of the job. Spending eight years at BT was also good fun and at least with the two most recent careers I did get a pension, but nothing except happy memories from racing.

When I look back, I really enjoyed working with Stephen in London as it was great to help him, a very special time for me working with my eldest son something which unfortunately my dad never got to do with me. My working life has been really good to me with all the different careers I have had which includes my gardening and my decorating.

Of course, the real bonus during my life was when I met the love of my life Elaine, we could not have been happier all these years. Our relationship has brought us three wonderful children who both Elaine and I love very much and are both so very proud of. Seeing them grow up, marry and have their own children is so special. We could not have wished for more wonderful grandchildren who we are also both so very proud of and love them all very dearly along with our 4 great-grandsons and great-granddaughter. All in all, I could not have asked for more, I have been truly blessed.

Printed in Great Britain
by Amazon

26503074R10106